MW01104545

Healthy, Abundant, And Wise

Stories by Inspired Individuals Who
Got There, Live There, and Discovered
Their Innate Power Along the Way

Powerful You!
PUBLISHING
Sharing Wisdom ~ Shining Light

HEALTHY, ABUNDANT, AND WISE
Stories by Inspired Individuals Who Got There, Live There,
and Discovered Their Innate Power Along the Way

Copyright © 2016

All rights reserved. No part of this book may be reproduced by any mechanical, photographic, or electronic process, or in the form of a phonographic recording; nor may it be stored in a retrieval system, transmitted or otherwise copied for public or private use–other than for "fair use" as brief quotations embodied in articles and reviews–without prior written permission of the publisher.

The authors of this book do not dispense medical advice or prescribe the use of any technique as a form of treatment for physical, emotional, or medical problems without the advice of a physician, either directly or indirectly. Nor is this book intended to provide personalized legal, accounting, financial, or investment advice. Readers are encouraged to seek the counsel of competent professionals with regard to such matters. The intent of the authors is to provide general information to individuals who are taking positive steps in their lives for emotional and spiritual well-being. In the event that you use any of the information in this book for yourself, which is your constitutional right, the authors and the publisher assume no responsibility for your actions.

Published by: Powerful You! Inc. USA
www.powerfulyoupublishing.com

Library of Congress Control Number: 2016938448

Sue Urda and Kathy Fyler–First Edition

ISBN: 978-0-99706612-8

First Edition May 2016

Self Help / Women's Studies

Printed in the United States of America

Dedication

*This book is dedicated to those who
follow their desires and open their hearts
to living in a space of well-being and abundance.*

Table of Contents

Insight

"No matter how difficult and painful it may be, nothing sounds as good to the soul as the truth."
~ Martha Beck, Author of Steering by Starlight

Foreword

Real transformation sneaks up on you. Maybe you have experienced that moment—that face-palm, slap to the forehead instant—when you realize you are in the middle of unplanned, unexpected, unpredicted life change. It can feel like all the air just got sucked out of the room when you figure it out because real transformation changes everything. What was can no longer be, not because you don't want it but because it just won't work in your life anymore. Who you were then is not who you are now… and the 'now' you cannot be put back into the smaller container of who you were 'then'.

We like to think that we can see what's coming and adapt proactively. We pride ourselves on managing all the spinning plates and bouncing balls while making a great living and having a great social life and staying fit and keeping a beautiful home and, and, and. The reality is that even if we see what's coming, we think we have enough time to address it as it comes 'later'… which usually arrives ahead of our schedule for it.

More often, we are so busy living our lives every day that we miss the signs that transformation is headed our way. There is never enough time for 'later'; the good news is that you can catch at least three signals of change when you know what to look for as you live your life.

One of the telltale signals of change is *restlessness*. It feels a bit like being a Lamborghini stuck behind a lawn mower. You are revved up with nowhere to go. You decide to go out but you don't know where you want to be—and it really doesn't matter because wherever you are is not 'it'. You want to change careers but you have no idea what you want to do. Ripping through your closet to donate everything is satisfying—until you realize you need clothes to wear and you don't know what your style is anymore anyway. A sense of restlessness is the pre-adrenaline rush that is preparing you for fight or flight until you figure out that there is a bigger reason for why you feel the way you do.

Another signal is *things ending around you*. Life chapters that close in your life—relationships, projects, jobs, kids moving out, old beliefs that don't make sense anymore—can signal you are changing. When you change, everything else changes. If you see everything else changing, it's time to look within. When things are ending, it is clearing space for new beginnings (aka, transformation). If you do not start your next phase intentionally, you leave yourself open to whatever change happens to be passing your way. That might look like a friend who has a traumatic break-up or a family member passes or a lover gets transferred to another city and you get sucked in to handle the details. When the cup of your life starts going empty, notice it and fill it with the life juice you want to experience.

And then there are repetitive challenges. These are yet another signal of change. When you are looping through the familiar scenery of any particular situation, like a 'discussion' with a loved one, going on a diet or dating the same not-right person—again, you are being gifted with the opportunity to identify the pattern and resolve it on your terms. If you do not step up to the challenge, you will experience that same situation again in the future but it will be bigger, badder, and bolder because it needs to get your attention. Do yourself a favor and see it in the moment so you can break the cycle before it breaks you. You do not need to suffer; you only need to wake up to your own life.

If you are fortunate enough to recognize any of these signals, you might be able to initiate change on your own proactively far in advance of life events making you change. Chances are that won't happen.

Most of the time we are not aware and so we get caught off-guard by life's unexpected circumstances. In retrospect, once we get through them, we can trace back to where we should have seen the signals and that somehow makes it easier to take our lumps and get on with it.

Far more profound are the transformations that happen in response to the chaotic nature of life as it happens—the things we cannot control. Your life partner is diagnosed with a significant disease. Your out-of-state father passes away and his house is condemned because he rented to a hoarder who is now squatting there and not even the bank will take it back. Your child made a lot of money right out of school but did not know how to manage it and had an undiagnosed mental condition and so went bankrupt and now lives on donations. You find yourself increasingly sick—and no doctor can diagnose what's going on—only to discover you unknowingly moved into a home with an aged black mold colony living in your air conditioner, compromising your health in innumerable ways. As amazing as they seem, these are all true stories that dragged the people concerned through rugged, seemingly senseless and unnecessary, transformations.

In the bigger picture, maybe there is a bigger purpose to this kind of transformation—the unwanted, unforeseen and undesirable circumstances that force the essence of your spirit through your cracks to pull you forward kicking and screaming into your next level of awareness. Looking back, would you choose your growth to be as it's been? Probably not. And yet, you will likely have to admit that the richest rewards have likely come from the most difficult situations.

Transformation looks like it happens on the outside but the reality is that it changes you from the inside. It's not what happens to you but how you handle it that determines your character and your quality of life. What will you do with the cards you have been dealt? This is the pivot point question that transformation offers IF you can step back to see it in—or at least after—the moment of change.

The stories you are about to read contain the pain and the power of real transformation. There is a special beauty that you will feel in witnessing each author's growth through their experiences into their 'now' self. Whether they thought they were ready or not, they have become more of themselves because of their journey. You will see life through their eyes for just a moment. You will likely agree that who they are now is all the more special for where they have been because of the reality of their transformation.

Even more, if you allow yourself to be in that moment with them through their story, you too will be changed.

Lynn Scheurell
Seer, Teacher, Writer
Las Vegas, NV

Introduction

Innate Power

Innate Power. There's nothing you can do to earn it. You can't buy it, barter for it, or steal it from someone else. You can't learn it or gather it. You can't grow it and you can't deny it—although many people try to.

Innate Power is something you're born with. It's already yours.

It's true. Every single individual on the planet has an amazing inherent power that is waiting to be tapped; and yet there are so many people who either never knew they had the power, thought they lost their power, or allowed it to be covered up by things like unworthiness, low self-esteem, lack of self-love, or the misconceived notion that they aren't good enough to wield such power. Nothing could be further from the truth.

Some people walk around every day with incredibleness bouncing around in their bellies, pouring from their hearts, and flowing through their veins. There is literally so much power in an individual that they could change their world on a whim, and many of them do.

Yet, many others walk around without the knowing or the acknowledgment of their personal power and in doing so squander the very essence of who they are.

Innate power is something that must be recognized by the individual who possesses it for it to have any meaning. The fact that *I know* you possess this power doesn't mean anything for how you conduct your life; it only matters that *you know* you possess the power, that you feel worthy of it, and that you tap into it and use it to manifest your dreams and become the amazing individual you are capable of being.

This inborn power shows up in as many different forms as there are people. Your power and my power may look quite different; maybe you have the power of artistry, musicianship, or creativity, whereas my power shows up as reasoning ability, mathematics, or culinary genius. The idea that power is defined as one specific trait, attribute, or quality makes no sense, because power is as personal as you and I.

The ability to recognize ones' own power is a gift that some people are born with. They know early on where they fit in or stand out in the world. I consider these people the lucky and blessed ones. They start on their path early on and move through life with confidence of their purpose and their place in society, their family, and even the world.

Most children have a sense of their innate power, and sometimes well-intentioned parents squash it in what they believe is the best interest of the child. They don't want their child to be *too different* than everyone else for fear of teasing, ridicule, and non-acceptance. They also believe the child can't possibly know better than they do what will make their child grow up to be a productive citizen and capable employee, spouse, parent, and friend. Unfortunately, this is often a disservice to the child, because dreams and gifts are put aside at the expense of conformity, and the true power of the individual must be uncovered later in life.

Other times personal power, strength, and unique abilities are simply not nurtured—again due to the need we have to 'fit in'. Although we are told to stand out, it is only approved of to a certain degree and often when there is evident success ahead if we follow the beat of our own drummer. Either way, the inborn power we have is frequently undeveloped, ignored, or blocked.

Fortunately, the gifts and power within continue to poke their way to the forefront, often through a longing, sometimes through the prompting of another awakened soul. No matter how it becomes evident to us, it is inevitable that each of us at some point recognize our innate power.

Many of the authors in this book write of just that—the rediscovery of their personal power. For many of them their power revealed itself in the form of a healing at a point when things were too much to bear. It was as if the answer to their pain or problems came forth from within, and in the allowing of it to come forth, they realized it had been theirs all along.

Others experienced a calling or a yearning. The little voice within became so loud that they could no longer resist the pull, and so they brought it forth willingly following every detail of the vision that was expressed. Much to their relief and delight they felt vibrant and whole, sometimes for the first time in their lives.

Yet others heeded the call grudgingly, for they may have been fearful of revealing their innermost desires, because the desires were so unfamiliar or so distinctive that they weren't fully understood and therefore not acknowledged. The truth is that our innate power shows up through these desires. The issue many individuals face with their power is that they have no experience or knowledge of what they are drawn to or that it is unlike anything they've ever seen or heard of, and so they are fearful of it or don't feel worthy of manifesting it.

Still others are fearful of the power they possess because it seems too magnificent to be theirs. And yet, as the authors tell it, the desire to experience and share their innate power is so great it must be met with inspired action. When this happens the bounty of life and the intrinsic power of the individual blossoms.

Perhaps nothing is sweeter than opening to your own power, harnessing it, and allowing it to flow through everything you do. If you ever experienced even a glimpse of this, you know the beauty and the allure, and you want to live in that space of power forever.

It is our wish and intention that the stories in this book will help you access your personal power either for the first time, or to step more fully into it. It is your birthright. It is within you. It is ready to be cultivated. May you feel it, may you honor it, and may you express it.

With deep gratitude and much love,
Sue

Sue Urda
Feel Good Guidess
Co-Founder of Powerful You! Inc.
A connections and empowerment company
powerfulyou.com

May You Discover
Your Innate Gifts...

And Use Them Wisely!

Growing in the Gap
Marilyn Bellantoni

I stood over the phone and watched my right index finger unsteadily press the series of numbers written on the pink post-it note stuck to the sweaty palm of my left hand. My entire body trembled as if hypothermic and the lump in my throat grew so large it threatened to cut off my breath. I regretted not having a chair nearby as my athletic legs turned to spaghetti beneath me.

After pressing the last number, I held my breath and heard the deafening drum of my heartbeat between each ring. The ringing stopped, then a raspy, somewhat familiar voice on the other end of the line said, "Hello." Like a cartoon caricature, I responded with an exaggerated gulp and an unsure, "Hello." An uneasy silence followed, three seconds that seemed like three minutes. Then the two of us spoke with each other for the first time in our lives. This was surreal. I was actually conversing with the woman who had given birth to me forty-two years earlier, then given me up for adoption. Within the first few minutes, we both let down our guards and set a date for meeting face to face. As it turned out, my birthmother lived just around the corner from my adoptive mother. In this single conversation, the blank canvas of my origins came to life.

The story began in 1960, when a single mother got pregnant with her fourth child. For three weeks after giving birth, she did all she could to take care of them. But four kids under the age of six were more than she could handle. Divorced from the father of the first three, she had no one to turn to, including the man she was dating, who had denied the existence of this baby both before and after she was born. Overwhelmed and barely able to put food on the table, she concluded that adoption was her only viable option.

My new parents were unable to have children of their own so adoption was the perfect solution for them. They loved me like their own flesh and blood. I asked for a baby brother and they adopted one for me. Life was good. When I was five years old, my mother spoke to me about being adopted. As she recounted the day they brought me home, she was sure to tell me how I was loved, wanted, and chosen. This moving story was also peppered with humor; apparently when my paternal grandmother first laid eyes on me she stated, "You must have really wanted a child."

"You were completely bald," my mom chuckled, "your feet were rotated backwards, and you were as skinny as a plucked chicken."

My physical shortcomings never compromised my parents' love, but the information they provided left some gaping holes that I filled with a false, negative narrative. I thought, "If I were lovable, my birthmother would have kept me. If I'm a good girl, I won't be abandoned. I was a mistake; I should never have been born. I don't deserve to be here."

Even though my parents loved me, I didn't believe I deserved their love. After all, I was a reject that at least two people—my birth mother and father—didn't want. Much of my teenage years were spent trying to prove my worth. I studied harder than necessary to get good grades, until my mother actually begged me to stop. And I carried it yet further. I fell in love with the sport of fencing and spent whatever time I wasn't studying perfecting my fencing skills. I became an accomplished fencer, all 4 feet 10 ¾ inches of me. Fencing became my refuge, the place where I knew I was good at what I did and there was no opponent too big or too powerful for me.

Eventually, I came to realize that I had become my own worst enemy. I'd allowed circumstances over which I had no control, to define my life and determine my worth. I spent years engaging in subtly self-destructive behavior, designed to punish myself for the legacy of secrets and shame surrounding my birth. I perpetuated that legacy by hiding my self-destructive behavior from everyone, even my therapist. One such behavior was nail-biting. I remember the day I started the habit. I was in the second grade and my brother was in kindergarten. He came home from school very excited about something he'd learned. I was thinking "alphabet", but instead he started demonstrating the art of nail-biting. I gave it a try and in no time at all, a seemingly harmless activity became a lifelong habit that lowered my self-esteem and confidence further. Although I grew up in a Polish and German household, the Italian has always been in my blood. How does an Italian talk if she's always hiding her hands, eh?

As the main character in my story about being unlovable, I embraced additional shame in my early teens. I had always been a short, skinny kid, but in between eighth grade and high school, I went from being flat-chested to well-endowed, practically overnight. This unforeseen windfall earned me ridicule from both girls and boys alike; some even labeled me a "slut." Being adopted already made me feel different but having such large breasts on such a short body made me look like a freak! How did I hate me? Let me count the ways. I didn't feel like I belonged anywhere, not even in my own body. However, I did receive a temporary fix when, as a college freshman, my mother suggested breast reduction surgery. I jumped at the chance to be able to wear clothes that fit me properly and have people look at my beautiful eyes rather than my over-ample breasts. My self-confidence soared for awhile after the surgery, but it was also yet another secret to keep. I lied to those who complimented my new look, telling them I had lost weight. Admitting the truth would just have confirmed the belief that no matter what I did, it would never be enough! Later on, I discovered that by keeping silent, I was reinforcing negative beliefs about myself. The silence and shame disempowered me and disconnected me from my authentic self.

In college, I engaged in the self-destructive behavior of excessive partying into the wee hours of the morning. At the campus pub my friends and I mastered Beer Drinking 101. I wore my poor sleeping habits like a medal of honor. "Look at me," I proudly proclaimed, "I can survive on three hours of sleep and that's without drugs." Heck, I fed my pet mouse better than I fed myself—he got the imported Swiss cheese while I subsisted on ramen noodles. Slowly but surely I was shortening my lifespan, killing myself, because I was still operating under the premise that I wasn't significant or lovable enough to take proper care of myself. After all, I didn't really belong here anyway.

The need to belong became a driving force, as I had spent most of my life not fitting in. My mother always said I marched to the beat of a different drummer. However, I lived a dichotomy of not wanting to be like everybody else, but at the same time, needing to fit in somewhere. This inner conflict reached its peak when after seven years of exclusively dating women, I started seeing the man I would eventually marry. With women, I fit in; I was part of that world. Dating a man put me in a world I thought I had left behind forever. Instead of feeling like, "Wow, I could be happy either way!" I found myself feeling like a fish out of water, like a stranger in a strange land. I was torn between the way I felt about the man in my life and the conviction that I was a lesbian. I was angst-ridden, unable to tolerate the fact that my black and white world was disintegrating into shades of grey. I'd fallen into a "gap" between opposing worlds, but it was in this gap that my growth began. The tug-of-war I was playing with myself caused the rope to fray until it threatened to snap. It wasn't until I gave the rope some slack that I was able to accept myself as a person who could love and be loved without limitations.

Learning to "grow in the gap" was mirrored in a ropes course I took when I was in my twenties. While attached "on belay" to a safety system of ropes and pulleys, participants climbed twenty-five feet into the air along a thick telephone pole with staggered spokes. Upon reaching the tiny platform at the top, you faced twin cables stretched across to a second platform about fifteen to twenty feet away. The lower cable served as a tightrope, aided by knotted ropes dangling about four feet apart along the length of the upper cable. The tall woman who went before me had no problem negotiating the course. Then it was my turn. I couldn't wait to climb up that pole and experience the exhilaration of being up in the trees, way above the rest of the participants. What I wasn't prepared for was the challenge posed by my short stature. Walking across that tightrope meant being willing to let go of one rope before getting a grip on the next one. I took a deep breath, released the fear, and forged on.

That ropes course provided a valuable lesson that has stayed with me to this very day. When you cling too tightly to something like a belief or a story about yourself, the only way to change is by letting go of the old story and reaching for a better one. You have to brave those moments in between when there's nothing to hold onto. You are the author; you are in charge. The tightrope is your life. Things may get shaky at times, but you always have a choice. You can cling to the rope that's keeping you where you are right now, or you can let go and move along the cable and see what tremendous things life has to offer you. When you're standing in the "gap" between ropes, this is when you are most vulnerable; this is where transformation occurs. New story, new identity, new life!

Now I have a husband and two beautiful daughters that I never would have had if I hadn't let go. For the past six years, through my health coaching practice, I have had the pleasure and privilege of helping other women let go of the stories and beliefs that hold them back, helping them find a home in their own bodies, courage and conviction in their own minds, and love and belonging in their own hearts.

ABOUT THE AUTHOR: Marilyn Bellantoni, better known as the "Short Coach with Tall Results" is an author, motivational speaker, and health and transformation coach. Through workshops, group programs, and speaking engagements, she has inspired thousands of women to know, love, and care for their own bodies, replace toxic habits and thought patterns with empowering ones, and "Stand Tall" with self-confidence and courage. Marilyn enjoys making memories with her two daughters, two dogs, two guinea pigs, and two fish, all female! Her husband is the grateful recipient of all that feminine energy—Bless his heart! Marilyn is a lifelong New York Mets fan.

Marilyn Bellantoni, CHHC, AADP, TCM
Ruby Fruit Holistics, LLC
rubyfruitholistics.com
marilyn@rubyfruitholistics.com
908-393-7205

Heron Earth
Following the Call
Nancy Fairchild

Signs, Guideposts, and Symbols

As I was pondering what on earth I would name this chapter—and what I wanted to share in it—a great Blue Heron flew directly in front of my path from the left-hand side. This was significant, as I learned a long time ago that throughout our lives there will be signs or guideposts to help us on our path. In my case they have always come in the form of animals, shapes, and colors. I would also have distinct feelings or just an unexplained "knowing." When I saw the heron, excitement shot through me, for I knew I was being guided by one of nature's messengers.

Heron's message is this: look deeper into aspects of your life. It teaches that grounding yourself in the earth and your spiritual beliefs will help you to discover emotional insights more clearly and quickly. The heron also advises you to be on the alert for opportunities so that you can quickly grasp them and move on. Thank you, Blue Heron!

The fact that he flew in from the left side was also important. I have learned from great spiritual teachers and personal experience that the left signifies a message of a feminine nature. It whispers of receptivity and the ability to create from our core, as well as our feelings and the messages they share with us. Femininity is also associated with the moon. Like the many phases of the moon, which are ever-changing and yet still part of the whole, so are our emotions. Emotion is the fluid currents coursing through our solid bodies and moving us ever forward. Yet forward movement will only occur if we allow, feel, and listen.

Magic in the World

As a child, I would wander through the woods around my home. I loved what I referred to as "being on the outside" because I felt safe and I trusted the way of this world. It was within this world that I could experience a total sense of freedom. It has been said that not all who wander are lost and this definitely described me! I loved nature and all of its wonders. It was the land of the Fairies and their magical kingdom of flowers, animals, trees, plants, minerals, lights, and shadows. The scents, sights, and sounds always seemed to be calling me. I could instinctively tune into them— utilizing what I now know as clairsentience, claircognizance, and empathic feeling. I would sit for hours talking to the plants, pretending to be one of them. Did it want to communicate with me that day? How did its leaves sit, hang or fall? How did it feel to be a plant? What did it feel like to be green? That was always the question for me—*how did it feel?* If I could get a sense of what "their feeling was," perhaps I could understand them and therefore "be" whatever it was I was feeling. At times, I could subtly sense a merging of myself and the object I was communicating with. The woods and the sentient beings living there taught me many lessons that I would need later on, such as sensing and trusting all the subtle nuances I detected and felt; listening with my heart and following with my feet; that communication comes from many places and in many forms; and, finally, that seeing is not believing but in believing you will see.

Descending into Distortion

Even while I was having all these magical experiences, I was also living in another, polar opposite world. In fact, most of the time I felt lonely and disconnected—like I didn't really belong to the people I lived with. It seemed they felt it too, often saying, "Oh that's just Nancy being Nancy!" I wasn't really sure what that meant, but I did know how it felt: like I was not enough and perhaps not even wanted.

As a way of coping and predicting what was gonna happen at home, I applied a technique I'd learned in the woods. Just as I dialed into the energy of plants and animals, I learned to dial into other people's energy systems. In doing so, I received deep insights into their emotional wants or needs. Along with these insights, I could also sense or feel things they were hiding from the outside world. Unfortunately, I would often confuse what was happening in real time versus what had yet to be expressed, which resulted in my blurting out things that were met with criticism or denial. Even worse, boundaries were blurred, if recognized at all, so that I was often unsure of where I began and others ended. This further instilled the feeling of being "crazy" and that it was not worth it to be me.

It was on the "inside" of my childhood home that I learned my physical body and its sensations could not be trusted. Feelings were unacceptable and not to be shared. This message was constantly reinforced in several ways. I was conditioned with statements like "You did not hear that!" or "NO, I did not see that and neither did you!" I also observed others who, to me, seemed to be in denial. One day a cousin came down into the cellar and there, behind the furnace, found her brother with his hand in my pants. "What are you doing?" she asked; then although it was very clear what was happening, she simply turned around and left! *Her sight must be wrong too,* I thought to myself. Thanks to this lack of validation, I quickly learned to tune out of my body in order to not experience the shame, fear, and embarrassment of being "caught" doing something that felt so disgusting and dirty to me.

Escapism

When I was ten years old, my sister Kim and my grandfather Pappy—both of whom I loved dearly—passed away. The deaths were sudden, relatively close together, and utterly devastating. I actually felt as though I'd lost three people, for my mother was so consumed with grief it was like she was not even present. Lost and alone, I even begged God to take me back home instead of my sister. I had always sensed discord here on the physical plane and would have been perfectly happy going to one of the more spiritual realms I knew existed.

One night shortly after my sister's death I lay in bed, wide-eyed and afraid. Kim and I had shared a bed and she would often soothe my fear of the dark by pretending she was a fairy, speaking in a high-pitched voice and flicking a light on the angled ceiling above our heads. How I wished she were there with me now! Suddenly, I saw a white, light-beam cross shining on the bedspread. At first I thought it must be a shadow, created by moonbeams hitting the window pane, but when I looked out the window there was no light at all. I wouldn't realize until later that I was being comforted by my sister in spirit and the fairy realm!

In the meantime, I was stuck on *this* realm, and in order to escape from all the feelings of loneliness, self-loathing, pain, and suffering, I started sneaking into my much older brother's bedroom to listen to his stereo and to drink his alcohol. I hated the taste of alcohol yet loved its effects. The loud music worked too! For the next twenty years I spiraled into the world of addiction. I had several drugs of choice—alcohol, marijuana, nicotine, food, relationships, people-pleasing, rescuing, and approval—and I used them all to shut off parts of myself. This also disconnected me from my power. The spiritual sense of wonder I'd felt in the woods was gone, replaced by vulnerability and victimhood. My experiences in life became distorted, unpredictable, and painful. I believed I wasn't connected to creating my experiences and could not alter or change them for many years. One month before my thirtieth birthday, I found myself not wanting to live any longer. It was in this moment of complete and utter despair that I was touched by grace and the miracle of recovery started to unfold its wings to me.

Doorways, Passages, and Footpaths

Over the course of my fifteen-year journey of recovery, I have learned many wondrous things. I learned to align my body, mind, emotions, and soul, one day at a time. For me, the first step was no longer engaging in addictive behaviors and instead doing things that supported my recovery. Once that alignment has occurred then the emotional self has the space to open up into and, eventually, the soul unfolds and shines. Through recovery, I realized that I no longer have to be led around by others' feelings or lack of boundaries. It is okay to release the old and allow the new. It has also allowed me to disconnect from states of despair and insanity in order to reconnect to other realms by looking deeper into the aspects of my life. It has taught me to ground myself deeply into this earth so that I may create from my core and yet remain fluid and ever-changing like the moon. Most importantly, I learned how to trust myself and my gifts from the Divine Source.

Today, it is safe for me to be feminine and receptive while trusting my feeling nature. I know that in order to keep this gift of recovery and connection to the Source steady, one must learn to shine brightly so that others who have blockages can see the light and gravitate to it. As an Empathic Healer, I use my abilities to help others to release the past and move on with ease. I empower people by helping them to integrate body, mind, and spirit while using various tools such as Reiki, Aura and Chakra Biofeedback, Numerology, Astrology, and Intuitive Readings. I awaken people and remind them to nurture themselves and to listen to the call of their own spiritual guides and messengers that step forward. For it is in responding to the call that one can see all the magic and miracles around us here on earth.

ABOUT THE AUTHOR: Nancy Fairchild is a certified Soul Realignment practitioner committed to empowering individuals by helping them align their free will and everyday life choices to the divine origination of their soul. To do so, she uses energetic tools such as the Akashic Records, Aura photography/biofeedback, Reiki, Clairsentience, Claircognizance, symbolism, crystals, and astrology, which allow her clients tap into their own innate power and gifts. Nancy is currently working toward a Ministerial Bachelor of Holistic Theology degree from the American Institute of Holistic Theology.

Nancy Fairchild
Love In Life Wellness
Rainbowhawk.com
Nancy@Rainbowhawk.com
607-259-9169

The Mystery of Transformation
Mayra Liz Sanchez

One sunny day in 2007, my friend Dana and I found ourselves browsing the unfamiliar markets of New York City's Chinatown. We were about to take a class at the Traditional Chinese Medicine World Foundation that was "guaranteed to help us lose weight and manage our stress". We had no idea what the class entailed, but what we read about The Dragon's Way™ program definitely intrigued us. After all, what female is not interested in losing weight and getting de-stressed? The next six weeks opened my eyes, mind, body, and spirit to a new understanding of health and energy. We learned a martial arts form named Wu Ming Qigong, followed a simple eating-for-healing plan, and were introduced to the Five-Element Theory, which is used to understand the interrelatedness of all things in the universe. At the end of the six weeks, Dana and I saw significant results and had gained a better understanding of this five-thousand-year-old healing practice. Physical symptoms I had endured for many years disappeared, my emotions were more stable and I felt more hopeful about my future.

A few months later, I received an email from the Foundation. They were offering training to become a Certified Dragon's Way Instructor. Though I was interested, I just could not imagine how or where this would fit into my life, given my Latin culture and professional background (not to mention the fact that my knowledge of Chinese culture and martial arts had been gleaned from watching a Bruce Lee movie!). The more my mind resisted, however, the more I felt called to do it. Once I took that faith-filled leap, my life changed. I became a full-time qigong student and trained in multiple self-healing programs, after which I was fortunate enough to work for the Foundation.

By the fall of 2012, I was ready to celebrate and spread the word about the unlimited healing possibilities available with qigong practice and Traditional Chinese Medicine (TCM) at our annual "Building Bridges" conference in Chantilly, Virginia. According to the Chinese Zodiac, 2012 was the Year of the Water Dragon and held great potential for transformation, mystery and unexpected events. *My* transformative opportunities had come in the form of an unexpected financial loss followed by the painful and rather mysterious breakup of a long-term relationship. Continued qigong practice, study, and application of the principles helped me put those experiences in perspective, let go of the past and move into a brighter future. I had no idea that my character, faith, and work would soon be sorely tested.

In preparation for the conference, I reached deep into the recesses of my closet for a traditional Asian-style, wine-colored dress with perfectly placed golden dragons and phoenixes. I was delighted to note that this fifteen-year-old impulse buy still fit me, as it had always inspired a certain feminine confidence that I have only felt a handful of times. It was also the perfect outfit to honor the year, my new attitude, and the work I was so passionate about.

I returned home on a natural high, not only because of the incredible and uplifting experience at the conference, but because Paula, one of my closest friends, was coming to visit for a week. She and I had met and instantly connected many years earlier while working for the same company in Manhattan. Not a native New Yorker, she moved back home soon after having a baby; however, despite the distance we had remained in constant contact. The weather was unseasonably warm when Paula arrived and it provided the perfect backdrop for visits to the museums, Central Park, and the theatre. Whispers of an approaching storm gave us pause, as did the sight of some neighbors placing sandbags in front of their doors. But for the moment at least there was not a cloud in the sky, and I continued to enjoy the weather and the joyful time spent reconnecting with my friend.

Two days before Superstorm Sandy hit, Paula and I were walking along the beach. I remember the sun being so warm, the breeze so light and the ocean so unusually quiet. The birds were scarce and I noticed more debris than I had ever seen on previous walks. Dead fish, garbage, horseshoe crab shells and driftwood littered the beach, and every now and then a strange smell would assault our noses. Still there was an odd beauty to it, and I pulled out my cell phone to take pictures. While snapping a photo, I got a call from an ex-boyfriend. His voice was anxious and he was asking if I had made "arrangements". When I asked him what he was talking about, he shared the reports of the impending storm and told me my neighborhood was to be evacuated. He even offered to have us all stay with him during the crisis. After thanking him, I ended the call and told Paula what he had said. As we continued our walk, I felt the anxiety starting to build in my gut. Suddenly, I saw a large cross built in the sand with flowers arranged at the bottom. I took that as an ominous sign.

The next day was a blur, as the whole household worked hard to prepare for the evacuation. By that point sandbags were so scarce that Paula and I decided to make our own. Along with my two daughters, we drove to the beach across the street and filled our bags with sand. Trying to lift the bags into the car was like an "I Love Lucy" episode, with the four of us struggling through the process and laughing at the ironic circumstances we found ourselves in. But somewhere between the jokes and the frenzied state of the neighborhood it became clear to me that our ability to prepare was limited. On the day of the evacuation we focused on taking the essentials to my ex-boyfriend's house and left our home in God's hands.

The day of the storm we stayed indoors, ate, took care of the pets, and watched TV to keep track of Sandy's activity. I spent a lot of time praying in silence. The trees shook violently and the rain poured all day. Still we slept well that night having shared a peaceful and warm day together. The next morning we went to survey the damage to my home, but as we approached the main street we saw that the police had closed off the neighborhood. As we parked the car and began the half-mile walk to my house, I noticed the cattails in the marshland. The mixture of light and shadow produced a sight that reminded me of a field of defeated soldiers after a long battle. The debris caught among them seemed like white flags signaling their surrender. Even after watching the news coverage, we were all surprised at the amount of devastation. The streets were wet and in some cases sunken, so each step had to be taken with extreme caution. Every house and storefront had been impacted and cars appeared in the most unlikely places, as if they had been flung about like toys. The damage left behind by the "Perfect Storm" was intense, extensive, and surreal.

I will never forget the shock of seeing my home for the first time. The entire first floor, including my home office, garage and utility space were destroyed, and it quickly became obvious we could not go back home any time soon. That day, October 30, 2012, a personal winter began for our family that increased in severity once the actual season began. As a single mom and head of the household, I struggled the hardest with being unable to control the circumstances and make our world safe again. November and December brought a mix of isolation, deafening silence, extreme confusion, agonizing self-pity, anger, and disappointment towards God, the police, insurance agencies, FEMA, banks, and anybody else I could think of. Some days I would sit for hours inside my frozen home, just observing myself and the neighbors trying to find a "new normal" under these volatile conditions. Inconvenience, high tension and frustration were a constant.

It took me six weeks to get the house ready for us to move back in. I then realized my "new normal" was one of sheer exhaustion, chest pain, panic, worry, and dread. My desperate attempts to think about the bright side and appreciate the positive things that did happen during this time failed miserably. In reaction to this traumatic event, deep rooted cynicism, fear, and anxiety revealed themselves. These negative thoughts and emotions were like spiritual termites, consuming my faith and threatening the very foundation of my being.

As the holidays approached, the fresh losses exacerbated the sadness I often felt around that time of year. I grieved for our lost Christmas tree and all the ornaments that each of us had selected over the years. I cried for the pictures and mementos from my children's childhood that I would never see again. The storm had washed away pages of our history and I feared that over time the memories would fade too. Even worse, my downward spiral was affecting my kids.

Somewhere in the darkness, a glimpse of light illuminated my mind and I remembered how to move on and let go of my past and present pain. I returned to being a Dragon's Way student and focused on making the wise choices that would ultimately rebuild my energetic foundation. A new phase of my life was beginning. I slowly became excited again and noticed my own heart, mind and spirit integrating and healing again. My perspectives about my own personal life changed dramatically. The adversity I experienced helped me mature spiritually, grow more adaptable and more determined to positively affect my community and the world.

When March came around, the repairs were nearly completed. I noted the narcissus growing in the window boxes that had been covered by ocean water. Naturally, life had found a way to continue. My heart sang and opened up to all the new beginnings around me. It was my moment to begin a new cycle too. It was then that I decided to take another leap of faith and pursue my old dream of entrepreneurship. With a mixed bag of emotions, I left the Foundation to launch S.I. Dragon Lifestyle on Staten Island. Today, my mission is to promote, educate, inspire, and encourage others to heal themselves using the extraordinary yet practical wisdom found in TCM and Wu Ming Qigong. With patience, courage, discipline, decisiveness and—most of all—faith it is possible to move beyond the survival stage and cultivate new levels of wisdom, abundance, and health. I know, because I am living proof!

ABOUT THE AUTHOR: Mayra Sanchez is the proprietor of S.I. Dragon Lifestyle; a Certified Dragon's Way™ Instructor; and Medical Qigong Practitioner dedicated to educating the public on the many health benefits of Traditional Chinese Medicine (TCM) and Wu Ming Qigong. A proactive, "do-it-yourself" kind of woman, she used TCM and qigong to rebuild her health after living with pain, depression and fatigue for over a decade and again after a major crisis in 2012. Her experiences inspired her to share her knowledge of the comprehensive holistic system and inspire others to embrace personal accountability in relationship to mind, body and spiritual health.

Mayra Liz Sanchez
S.I. Dragon Lifestyle
sidragonlifestyle.com
sidragonlifestyle@gmail.com
347-528-1895

Rise to the Occasion
Robin David

The morning of Sunday, May 3, 2015 was a glorious one. As usual, I woke up early to affirm the promises of Father God (Abba) over my life and family, then proceeded to get ready for church. The sermon was especially powerful that day and inspired me to do something outside my normal routine, so afterwards, I decided to take a drive to my daughter's home in the country. She and I talked for a while, then I returned home to prepare for a meeting back at the church later that evening. I kept noticing what a gorgeous day it was, the way the sun's rays touched everything with golden light and the birds sang *Hallelujah* in perfect harmony. I took a moment to reflect on the beauty of life, as Jayla, my youngest daughter and Willie, my youngest son, came to sit with me on the patio. I remember saying to them, "We are at a crossroads in our lives. We have to make good choices." It seemed as though everything was falling into place.

I was feeling so alive as I walked into the church for my meeting, but before I could sit down and get settled, my phone rang. The sound was blaring—it seemed like the loudest ring I'd ever heard and drew every eye in the church in my direction. Embarrassed, I grabbed my phone from my bag and was surprised to see that it was Jayla.

"Hello!?" I whispered, thinking that perhaps she had forgotten about the meeting.

"Mom!" she said, her voice nearly shrill with fear, "Willie was shot!"

Before my brain could even process what she was saying, I was on my feet and moving to the back of the church, where my friend was sitting.

"Please! Give me a ride home!"

At her questioning look I explained what I knew.

"Don't worry, Robin," she said as we got in the car, "He is going to be fine."

As we approached my neighborhood, I was feeling hopeful, expecting that Willie would indeed be okay. I could not conceive anything else. Then I saw the piece of yellow police tape across my backyard, attached to a tree, and an uneasy feeling began to grow within me.

"What does the yellow tape mean? What's wrong? My son, my son!"

Again, my friend told me not to worry, but it was getting harder to stay positive.

When I walked into the house, Jayla rushed to me and said the emergency response team had air-lifted Willie to a hospital forty miles away.

On the drive over there, I thought about the conversation I'd had with Willie just that morning. He had told me that there were many toxic people in his life and he didn't want to be affiliated with them anymore. Then, with a sincerity I had never heard from him before, he confessed, "Mom you were right." In the past, when people asked about Willie, I would say, "He is building his testimony." I thought he would grow up to be a preacher. I was sure he would survive this gunshot and live to tell the world his story. Despite the circumstances, I was not going to let doubt overcome me. There was still hope.

I kept that cheerful attitude as I sat beside my immediate family in the hospital waiting room, and acknowledged that I serve the Creator of all; the One that will never fail me. I held onto hope when after what seemed like forever a nurse came in and asked us to follow her to the third floor. But as we exited the elevator I got that sinking feeling in my gut again. *God, I've always trusted You. I've always believed in You. Please don't tell me that my son is gone.* When we got to the door, they ushered us in, barricading the door behind us. They wanted to "consult" with us, they said.

When they told me my son had passed away, I didn't believe it; I just stood there in a complete state of shock. The tears came later, and it seemed as though they would never end. All night long, I cried; I cried until there were no more tears and all that came out were dry, agonized sobs. As a mother I understood that each of my children showed a different aspect of my character, and in losing Willie I felt I had lost a part of myself. "Did you not hear me, Lord?" I kept asking, until I fell into an exhausted sleep. The next morning, I sensed a presence by my bed, extending its hand to me, and I knew without a doubt that it was an angel. "We need you to get up," the angel said, "Your Heavenly Father will never leave you or forsake you. You will hold your head up. You will bottle up your tears and live your purpose today."

The last thing I wanted to do was get up; in fact, I never wanted to get out of bed again. But from that moment on, God began sending my dear family and friends, even people I had never seen before, to my aid; they encouraged me, loved me, helped me smile and confirmed the message of the angel.

After two days, I was finally able to eat—it was just fruits and vegetables at first, but it was the first steps on the road to recovery. One bite at a time. One phone call at a time. One prayer at a time. I continued this way for the next few months. I didn't keep track of the minutes, hours, or even days; everything still seemed like a painful blur. Yet I continued to take care of myself, eating healthy, working out at the gym, mediating and—as always—praying. The tragedy had also allowed me see who my support system was— friends, family, and of course, Abba.

I came to realize that this soul-shattering loss had forced me into an awakening—an unfamiliar place full of sorrow as well as a strange sense of excitement. I had been through the worst thing a mother could go through, yet I was still here and God was at my side. This gave me a confidence I had never experienced before, and allowed me to know and embrace the true value of life. The only way I could go from here was up! I began to forgive myself for past failures, and heard the voice within telling me, "You will rest in a place of peace and humility." Too loud to deny, gentle enough to accept, this was an opportunity for true healing, to learn how to love myself unconditionally, as Abba loves me.

In losing Willie, I learned firsthand what it was like for our Heavenly Father to give His only begotten son Jesus Christ so that the sins of the world could be forgiven. This is easy to scoff at if you've never had to give up the thing you hold most dear for the well-being of others, but once you do you understand that forgiveness, even in the midst of our worst suffering, leads us to more abundant and fulfilling lives. Forgiveness releases anger and allows healing in all circumstances—whether it is the loss of a job or a home or a loved one. We must embrace forgiveness before we can love ourselves and our lives again. For me, that meant forgiving my son's killer. I won't lie—it was excruciatingly difficult. I would take one step forward and three steps back. But eventually I realized that each and every tear was cleansing me of my past and preparing me for a new, better future. Without forgiveness I could have never moved onward and upward.

Today, I am in the most fulfilling place of my life. I am no longer a caterpillar, surviving one meal to the next, nor am I in my cocoon, needing to be sheltered from the elements of life. I have developed a colorful set of heavenly wings and gracefully blossomed into the beautiful butterfly I was chosen to be. I see that I am, with the infinite power within me, the co-creator of my destiny. Now I understand it's not about getting mired in the problems in our lives but finding power in the solutions.

I still miss Willie every day, yet I take comfort from the knowledge that he is in a better place. I am also grateful for my other four healthy, amazing children I can encourage and support. Through it all, Abba has continued to show me that He indeed is a provider. He reassured me that I am a powerful woman, an amazing mother and that my life has purpose. Each day, as I move forward toward my goals, I can hear my son's voice, saying, "I am so happy for you, Mom. I am celebrating you." He is my guardian angel, reminding me that there is no challenge in life that can steal my joy, my purpose and my peace of mind.

We all define our circumstances, they don't define us. Now is the time to rise to the occasion of fulfilling your purpose. Refuse to let people or things stop you from trusting the Almighty One within you. Realize that you are purposed into life to be powerful and that you are more blessed than you can imagine. Forgive others willingly. Make a profound effort to appreciate the value of the relationships you hold close to your heart. Tomorrow is not guaranteed, but now is more than enough time, not only to say "I love you," but to show it. Let your faith beam like a shining light. Serve others with a cheerful heart; let the world know you are here to love and be loved. Make a conscious effort to be alive and aware. Never settle for the ordinary; be encouraged to experience life outside your comfort zone. Don't be ashamed of your faith, who you are and *whose* you are. Stand out and do the right thing by any means necessary.

ABOUT THE AUTHOR: Robin David is a proud wife, mother and grandmother with a loving and supportive family. Her hobbies are golfing and traveling. Robin is a Healing and Wholeness speaker, facilitator, coach, and author who empowers women to live in their truth. In the early 1990's she opened a full-service nail salon and quickly developed a reputation as one to turn to for invaluable beauty tips and, when needed, a spiritual shot in the arm. This need inspired her to start Love U, L.LC, a company committed to helping women of all ages discover their inner beauty and achieve what she refers to as sacred balance. Today, Robin likens her work to "polishing people instead of nails."

Robin F David
Healing and Wholeness Speaker, Author, Coach
RobinFDavid.com
robindavid09@gmail.com
615-587-7239

Why Me?
Donielle Mills

"Magic," Paulo Cohelo wrote, "is a bridge between the visible and the invisible." I could not agree more. Once upon a time I was a lost soul. I had trouble conceiving a child. The challenges of motherhood, the death of a loved one, and divorce rocked my world. My son was diagnosed with Tourette's syndrome, and I with breast cancer. But I have learned that aside from their obvious challenges, these experiences contained gifts and lessons with a common thread: MAGIC. I believe this magic exists throughout the universe—in every person, place, and thing. It can be used to transform our stories—if only we are willing to cross that "bridge" every now and then.

My son was just six when he was diagnosed with Tourette's. I needed help to accept, embrace, and move on so I could then help him and our family do the same. When I asked the universe wholeheartedly for help, the following "poem" came flowing out of me. I repeatedly read it to my children and we all found it deeply healing. Keep in mind that this isn't just about Tourette's or about each of us being different and special. It isn't only about *my* story and *my* family. It's about life and its mysteries.

I feel that everything that happens in life is about all of us— every person, every place, and every thing. We are all connected. As you read this poem, plug in your own story and try to connect with your inner child. Try to take at least one step onto the "bridge of magic." By the end of the story you just might find that you have crossed to the other side.

Why Me?

There are many feelings that all people feel.
No matter what the feeling, it feels so real.
Anger and hurt name only two.
Confused, scared and sad make it a few.
While perfectly fine to feel all of these feelings.
It can also be helpful to find ways of dealing.
Things can get hard and things can get tough.
But just when you think you've had quite enough,
Feel all of your feelings, let them all out.
Then look at them differently and move on without doubt.

We have all asked the question, why me?
We wonder, how could this happen, how could this be?
Sometimes the answer is given to see.
Other times it's meant to remain a mystery.
Something very important, know this for sure,
This is a lesson on seeing things differently and opening new
doors.
Let's start by opening your heart and expanding your mind.
Life will be much more enjoyable and much more kind.
Here are some magic glasses. Put them on right away.
They will help you see differently in more than one way.
These glasses are not only special, magic and free,
But invisible too - for them you can't see.
Put them on go ahead, it may seem a bit weird,
To believe in something unseen we've surely all feared.
You'll have to practice each day with these new glasses of yours.
You'll see clearer than ever and be touched deep to your core.
Today's the first day. It will get easier with time.
Here's an example to follow, nothing short of sublime.

It's about a boy that suddenly was very confused.
His body kept twitching, leaving him far from amused.
Twitching and sniffing, moving that way and this,
He got headaches and muscle aches, you get the gist.

"What's going on, what's this about?
I don't like this at all," the boy shouted out!
The only way to get answers is to ask it right out.
"Why me Universe?" Let's find out….

"Why me?" asked the boy. "Why do I twitch?"
"Have I done something wrong? Did I flip the wrong switch?
Please tell me, great Universe, what is the reason
For each twitch, sniff and eye blink? They're not very pleasing!"

"What are these movements and sounds, you wonder?
Though not a bug, they are called tics," Universe replied in a
voice like thunder.
"To answer your question, why they exist….
"Keep those magic glasses on. You'll need them for this."

Earth chimed in and said with a smile,
"The tics that you have are important, dear child.
Each time you tic you send energy my way.
That energy stays close and travels far, far away.
It touches trees and animals and peoples the same.
Faces not only smile but release shame and blame.
Each tic that you have also helps people cry,
With every sad blink that's held in their eyes.
Each tear that comes down makes their cheeks nice and soft,
Making room for their happiness that's waiting aloft.
Each movement you make digs a new hole,
For a tree to be planted - one with a soul.
Each sound you produce calls the animals near.
It tells them they are heard and important, you hear?"

Sky answered next with a big booming voice.
"Each tic that you have although not by choice,
Lights up a new star and keeps the clouds moist.
Each time that you twitch the sun stays ablaze.
Bringing light, life and warmth to each of our days.
You keep the moon smiling down on us and shining so bright,
To light up the way for our journeys at night."

Mother Earth added, "You did nothing wrong.
We need you the way you are – perfect and strong."

The boy shivered and felt a chill.
He wrapped his arms around himself and stood very still.

Whoosh, whoop and howl the **Wind** blew in strong.
"If you think tics are bad I'll tell you you're wrong.
Each tic that you have keeps my gusts going.
For without my gusts I would not be blowing.
If I am not blowing, things would not be the same.
No leaves would be falling or dancing like rain.
There'd be no cooling breeze, no whistling heard.
No opt for green energy, my how absurd."

 "Then there's me," **Fire** said as he hissed, danced and crackled.
"I learn my movements and sounds from you," he cackled.
"If I were not here think of all the things that'd be missing.
Like light, warmth and energy, I'm not for dismissing.
You've taught me all that I know from these tics, don't you see?
If I weren't hissing and moving I wouldn't be me."

With the warmth of Fire's words the boy began to relax.
He looked up at the sky with wonder while lying on his back.

Suddenly, the skies opened up.
As the **Rain** came down he held out a cup.
"The clouds you keep moist with each tic that comes forth,
Brings water to all for all that it's worth."
"All living things need water, for sure.
Can you tell me why or shall we explore?
We need water to grow, to swim and to drink.
You help fill the oceans - how great, don't you think?
Each reservoir, lake, river and pond
Is so grateful to you and I'm sure very fond.
You shower the Earth with water and peace,
A rainbow of colors each time you release."

 "Remember this too," Universe said.

"On the days that the tics seem way too, too much,
When they make you feel crummy and yucky and such,
Get lots of good rest and dream lots of good dreams.
These dreams may reveal it's not as bad as it seems."

The boy drew in a deep breath and let it out slowly with ease.
He melted into the earth like the roots of the trees.

Mother Earth had more to say.
"That's a long answer filled with interesting verse,
To the question you asked, 'Why me, Universe?'
It seems that these tics play an important role
In keeping the Universe going and connecting each soul.
You were chosen to help, to guide and create.
You have something special about you, deep and innate.
We all do, you see? We each have our own 'thing'.
This thing or that thing and all in between."

The boy was glad he asked, "Why me?"
He hoped others would too, if they needed to see.

"Whatever your thing," said Universe, "whatever your part,
It may seem such a problem right from the start.
The problem can change, the problem can shift.
The magic glasses can show you a lesson and gift.
Not a gift like a bike, a doll or toy car,
But a gift that shows how important you are.
There is no one like you on earth to be found.
You and your 'thing' are important in helping the world go
'round."

Now very comfortable the boy fell asleep.
Mother Earth sensed more questions buried so deep.

"How long will you have this role do you ask?
How long will you be fulfilling these tasks?
Any questions you have don't hold them inside,
Ask yourself and the Universe, both wonderful guides.
Use all of your senses, answers aren't always heard.

They can be tasted or smelled, felt or seen in a word.
Also, be patient. Answers may not come right away.
They are there to be discovered on a magical day!"

Universe closed his eyes for a rest.
He first finished his story – one of his best.

"So what do you think? Aren't these glasses so cool?
Don't things look much better and not nearly as cruel?
Keep them, they're yours, forever to wear,
For the times when you're sad or you've had a great scare.
When you are mad, confused or distraught,
Your new magic glasses can transform every thought.
If one day you don't have them don't worry at all.
If they're gone, lost or broken you surely won't fall.
Imagine them on. Pretend they are there.
They're magic remember? No need for a pair."

Mother Earth took a deep breath. She was oh so pleased.
Another gift and great lesson shared on the breeze.
The breeze of the Universe blowing all through the lands
These lands are connected, all holding hands.

The End (or Beginning!!!)

I have read that the earth says much to those who listen. I listened. I heard everyone and everything, realizing the Oneness of it all. There is no "Me". There is only "Us." So really the question is, "Why Us?" The answer is, "Because."

My magic glasses then helped me to see my cancer as a part of me—a friend. I didn't want to "fight it" or "beat it". I chose to help it do whatever it came here to do—a work in progress.

Magic glasses, should you choose to put them on, can be your "bridge"—your connection to everyone and everything—your connection to a more healthy, abundant and wise life. *POOF* - just like that!

ABOUT THE AUTHOR: After leaving a career working with

cardiac patients to be a stay-at- home mom, Donielle Mills continued to nurture her other passions, including authentic human connection, looking at life through magic glasses and trying to live a more genuine and simple life. Donielle is currently channeling these passions into *Ohiyesa*, a new business with a warrior's mission. In offering small, personal, down-to-earth gatherings, she will guide discussions and hands-on exercises on how connection is lost and how to get it back. She hopes to share and empower others to believe in magic, build bridges and reconnect, most importantly to self, then to others and to our planet.

Donielle Mills
Ohiyesa
ohiyesa.net
dmills@ohiyesa.net
732-272-3607

Awakening to Love
Carey Cloyd

A few weeks after graduating from a master's program in Counseling Psychology, I drove with a friend from Denver to San Francisco. I would be staying with a couple of college friends at one of their parent's place while the three of us looked for an apartment together. My friend's mom had invited me to an event for a non-profit that helps indigenous tribes in the Amazon retain their land and culture in the face of opposition by oil companies and other industrial interests. On my way there, I noticed that I felt like I was on mushrooms, though I had not ingested anything—an experience that seemed odd and yet enjoyable at the same time. One with all, loving, open, spacious, and free, I walked along the pavement from my parked car to the address I had been given. I heard lively music as I approached, and at the corner of a nearby street, I noticed two colorfully dressed South American musicians beckoning participants inside.

One of the speakers that day was a shaman, who I was somewhat surprised to find was a white man from a corporate background. After the program ended I waited to speak with him so I could learn more about him and share my experience. He noted my altered state and offered to take some negative energy out of the back of my head, which he did with a few simple movements of his hands. I had recently read Eckhart Tolle's *The Power of Now* and the shaman shared with me that in a few weeks' time he would be teaching at a conference in Florida featuring Eckhart. I ended up flying across the country to attend and was exposed there to Byron Katie, a woman who teaches a simple and powerful inquiry into stressful thoughts. This exposure was my first taste of nondual teachings which would become much more prominent in my life some years later.

The experience lasted about two weeks. At points, the influx of energy was so strong that I did not feel the usual need to sleep or eat, though I continued to do so (albeit more moderately) as I did not wish to alarm my housemates and companions. There was an immense feeling of love and bliss, and a powerful realization that while circumstances may appear troublesome to the mind, on a deep level, ultimately all is well. Without fully recognizing the signals at the time, I began to be aware that when I am not in alignment with Truth, I experience disharmony in my body. With time, this capacity to sense and listen to disharmony in my body would grow significantly and continues to be an ongoing practice.

In the aftermath of this experience, my mind struggled to understand what had happened to "me" (my idea of "myself"). I felt as if my world had been made of Lego pieces and had somehow been turned upside down—the Legos had come undone and fallen into a pile on the floor, and "I" (an image of "myself") had come to while everyone around me carried on as usual, without even noticing that anything had changed?!?!! While I was aware that my experience might be misunderstood as unreal or "crazy," I also knew on some fundamental level that what I had experienced revealed underlying truths about existence. Basically, I realized that everything I had ever thought was untrue—that my thoughts typically construct a false reality, a story of a separate self at odds with or a victim of life. Thoughts can be more like a house of cards that can fall, revealing the illusion of substance they seem to create. They are in fact Nothing—simply movements of energy within the vast Wholeness of Being. Thoughts are certainly helpful to communicate, yet they need not be taken as or mistaken for Reality. As Rupert Spira writes, "Thought does not and cannot know Reality, and yet it is made of it."

I had previously been on a track of "Get a PhD; get married; have kids;" now I felt like an explosion had occurred, derailing the train. "I" could not just get right back on the same mental train tracks and continue on the journey as before. It felt a bit as if "I" had been catapulted into outer space, yet at the same time I was walking around on the surface of the earth just as before. My sense of myself had begun to shift from being a separate self—a person simply living out a certain existence that will end when the body expires—to being an expression of the Infinite, not bound by time or space and yet appearing within them.

I had some money from the death of my birth mother, and I used that to support myself for a time. I volunteered in Los Angeles at the international headquarters of the meditation group I was in: the Self-Realization Fellowship founded by Paramahansa Yogananda. I was moved to interview with their ashram (monastic) committee to learn more about their offerings. While they did not initially give me any guidance regarding the experience, they eventually suggested that I write it down for myself, as it seemed my mind was having doubts about its significance and validity. My sharing this story here is partly an outgrowth of that recommendation. I felt alone and unusual at the time, not yet having come across anyone who had been through a similar experience, or who even seemed to know firsthand what I was talking about. I did find a pamphlet written by a deceased disciple of this teacher who described an experience with similar elements, and I recall that being comforting to me.

The ashram interview committee gave me some sage advice, suggesting that since their path is one of meditation and activity, I resume the job search I had put on hold in the wake of this experience. I soon learned of a prospective job as a counselor in an Adolescent Day Treatment program (a specialized school for high school students with Severe Emotional Disturbances). As this setting was the same type in which I had done my initial training while in graduate school in Colorado, I was very excited to be involved with a similar program in California. During the interview, I noticed two of my guru's books on the supervisor's desk and when I asked about them, he said that the author was one of significance for him. I took this as a sign that I was in the right place and readily accepted the position.

In part, my interest in being of service as a monastic was an immense sense of gratitude for what had been revealed. Looking back on it, my inner world had radically altered (thoughts in general, myself, others, the world—seen to be ultimately formless and expressions of indivisible Love), and I may have naively assumed that my outer world would also radically change as a result. As it turns out, my calling to be a psychotherapist had remained and there was not a need or call to change my external circumstances.

In the meantime, I began meeting with a therapist recommended by a friend from my meditation group. Later on, I was drawn to go to a workshop with this same friend that happened to be being taught by a colleague of our therapist. I found myself very drawn to the teacher's style of working and he eventually became a mentor. In my initial meeting with him, he gave me language for what had happened, describing it as an "awakening" or "opening" experience. I was enormously relieved that someone had finally articulated what had taken place, and was able to understand and provide guidance about it. A couple of years later, I transitioned from seeing clients at the school to working at a low-fee community counseling center that provides transpersonal and somatic training to its therapists. My mentor supervised my work with clients there, providing professional training for which I am very grateful.

It has now been over twelve years since this awakening, and it continues to have a profound impact on how I experience myself. I am working as a psychotherapist in private practice, including co-coordinating an annual conference on Nondual Wisdom & Psychotherapy. The conference was initially co-founded and coordinated by my mentor who continues to be involved in an advisory capacity. I have also been drawn to a nondual teacher named Adyashanti, whose wife Mukti studied the teachings of Paramahansa Yogananda for many years. I enjoy the fact that Mukti represents a living bridge between these two lineages that are so meaningful for me. I have been drawn to pursue studies in energy work and bodywork that have greatly facilitated my growth and development—both personally and professionally. While I am open to being married and having kids, as well as getting a PhD, life has not moved in those directions. I continue to enjoy being physically active through ultimate Frisbee, hiking/backpacking, yoga, dance, and field hockey.

In the spiritual circles that I am currently involved with, I regularly witness fellow beings awakening to our True Nature, which has normalized and continues to normalize this occurrence for me. I continue to receive professional support for the trauma I experienced as an infant (my mother took her life while experiencing post partum depression after my birth). I meet together often with spiritual teachers and sangha (community), and regularly attend meditation retreats to deepen my remembrance of our True Nature as beings of Light and Love. In each moment, I am invited to inquire into any thoughts, feelings, or sensations that experience themselves as separate from this divine radiance that is our birthright and home. I invite you to do the same!

ABOUT THE AUTHOR: Carey Cloyd, MFT is a psychotherapist with a private practice in San Francisco and Marin County, California. She has been a counselor since 2000, with a regular meditation practice throughout. She initially studied the spiritual teachings of Paramahansa Yogananda and then was drawn to those of the nondual teacher Adyashanti. In her work with clients, Carey draws primarily from her trainings in Hakomi, EMDR and The Work of Byron Katie. She has served as co-coordinator for the Nondual Wisdom & Psychotherapy conference since 2009. In her free time, she enjoys hiking, yoga, and dance.

Carey Cloyd
Carey Cloyd Counseling
careycloyd.com
careycloyd@yahoo.com
415-488-6854

Are You Allergic to the 21St Century?

Maggie Poetz

Imagine one morning, you wake up and stumble to the bathroom to wash the sleep off your face, just like you do every other day. But this time when you look in the mirror, instead of seeing a beautiful face and smile, you see an ugly, bloated, barely recognizable version of yourself staring back at you. Your skin is sagging and splotched with red, and your hair is falling out in clumps. Now imagine you have no idea what is causing it.

I hadn't been feeling well for some time. My mind was foggy, and everything from my favorite foods to laundry soap caused me to break out in hives. I experienced uncontrollable itching all over my body, and a burning sensation in my mouth, tongue, and nose, as if someone was rubbing a jalapeño pepper on my skin. I also had chronic fatigue and skyrocketing blood pressure. But that morning, as I stood horrorstruck in front of my bathroom mirror, it truly hit home.

Two movies immediately came to mind—"The Boy in the Plastic Bubble" and "The Elephant Man"—and I knelt on the floor, sobbing and praying, asking God for guidance. All the doctors had done was prescribe steroids that, in addition to everything else, caused me to gain weight. At one point my neck was so swollen I looked like a linebacker for the NFL.

I couldn't believe this was happening to me. As a child I was blessed with good health and spent lots of time playing outdoors in the fresh air. If I wasn't running, horseback riding, sailing, or swimming, I was rolling on the ground with Sam, my beloved golden retriever.

My true passion, however, was creating things. After graduating with a bachelor's degree in Fine Arts, I continued my education at the Art Institute of Fort Lauderdale and became a professionally licensed Interior Designer.

My first interior design job was for a mega yacht builder in Fort Lauderdale. The boatyards, with the smells of varnish, fiberglass, and resin glues, reminded me of sailing with my father, a retired Navy Captain and boat builder.

Later, I began a career with a high-end residential design firm in Palm Beach. With so many homes to help create and remodel, this was even more exciting to me than the yachts. I travelled, went to furniture shows and rummaged through all sorts of warehouses looking for unusual finds. I also had a wonderful life and three furry "kids": Sandy Paws Surfer Girl, Savannah, and Marlin Blue. Life was very good!

Then one day, while in New York City on a job, my heart started to jump out of my chest and my entire body started to itch. Knowing something was wrong, I reluctantly left the job site and went to the ER. After running some tests, the doctors assured me that it was just my blood pressure and I should get on medication as soon as I got home.

When I returned to Florida things only got worse. After one especially long day at the office I felt myself growing increasingly weak. Breathing was difficult, and I was itchy, anxious, and felt bloated from head to toe. Yet no one else could see that my body was under attack.

I went from doctor to doctor, but found no solutions. All the blood tests came back normal, yet I instinctively knew they were not looking in the right places. They on the other hand decided I had a psychological problem. To appease me, they prescribed a round of steroids, which was nearly as bad as the illness itself, causing me to put on weight and get that "linebacker neck." Stressed and overwhelmed, I started to believe that the doctors were right. Was I losing my mind? Was I dying from some mysterious disease? I began writing in a journal each morning, keeping track of my symptoms, trying to remind myself that I was sane and that this was really happening to me.

The world looked amazingly the same, but my part in it had changed. It seemed like everywhere I went, every time I took a breath, it made me sick. Whereas I had always enjoyed going out with friends and colleagues, I now found myself cancelling plans with them, often at the last minute and without an explanation, at least not one they could understand. Most of the people I knew did not take my illness seriously, and some were even offended when I became ill in their homes or by the perfume they wore. Imagine the worst hair day you've ever had—that dread of being seen in public—and you'll have a small sense of what I felt.

My mysterious illness was also affecting my home life. After a long day at the office I'd drag myself home, barely able to function, then I'd wake up the next day feeling like I'd been out all night drinking. My husband was becoming desperate too. The woman he loved was literally falling apart in front of his eyes. Not knowing what else to do, he suggested we go on a cruise.

I decided to use this time to gain perspective on what was happening to me. Sure, it felt strange, sitting on the lido deck, reading *Homes that Heal, Could Your Home be Making You Sick?* After all, I was supposed to be on vacation!

But discomfort soon turned to excitement when I realized that the book was describing every symptom I had. And it wasn't just my home either; in fact, my work environment appeared to be the primary culprit. I had spent years around toxic elements, first in the boating industry, then in the houses I helped build and remodel. In truth, I had been around chemicals ever since taking all those art classes in college. The cumulative effect on my immune system had led to a case of Multiple Chemical Sensitivity.

MCS is a serious, progressive neurological disease that develops as a result of the bombardment of chemicals in our everyday environment. These include personal hygiene products such as shampoos and soaps; pesticides on food and in gardens, chemical cleaners; paints; new carpets; and building materials. The lovely scent your friend wears can launch a full-blown assault on your immune system. Even that plug-in air freshener that smells like "fresh rain" or the "ocean breeze" may just be the straw that breaks the camel's back.

In the acute phase, any exposure to these elements can cause MCS sufferers to experience a myriad of symptoms similar to those of autoimmune disorders. They include but are not limited to lethargy and fatigue, difficulty concentrating, anxiety, muscle aches, memory problems, digestive problems, joint pain, extreme headache, tenseness, insomnia, depression, eye irritation, dizziness, chest pain, high blood pressure, nausea, rashes, and hives, and burning sensations.

Given the many triggers and symptoms, MCS is very difficult to diagnose. This means your well-meaning doctors, friends, and colleagues might start to think this is all in your head. Feelings of loneliness, desperation, and isolation become a normal way of life.

That book changed my life. My symptoms were real— they had a name, and others were dealing with them. Now armed with knowledge, I sprang into action. I took stock of everything in my home and work environments that were making me sick, then I called my allergist and told him I was stopping the steroids.

The next step was to purify my house and body. I removed all toxic cleaners and began using filtered water. I got rid of everything that produced dust and/or mold. I threw the windows open whenever I could and got air sanitizers. I started wearing clothes made only of organic cotton. I also started doing things to calm my body, mind, and spirit—grounding to the earth by taking walks barefoot; praying and meditating; exercising and paddle boarding. I played with my dogs and spent time with my husband. I also took up "hot yoga" and found it helped me immensely. The yoga studio is heated to over one-hundred degrees, which causes profuse sweating. Later, I learned that saunas are one of the treatments for MCS, as the perspiration detoxifies the body.

My next challenge was what to do about work. I loved my career as an interior designer, but I couldn't continue to do it at the cost of my health. Fortunately, I was able to work from home, which I did part time while I recovered. I also went back to school and obtained a certification as a Bau Biology & Ecology Consultant from the International Institute for Building-Biology & Ecology. Later, I passed the USGBC exam to become an Accredited Professional in Leadership Energy Efficient Design (LEED) from the United States

Green Building Council.

It has taken me ten years and counting to regain my health, and it is an ongoing process. I am still chemically sensitive, but thankfully I am no longer at the "emergency" level I once was. It will probably never go away completely, but I have learned to listen to my body and get out of environments that may lead to a flare-up. If I do start to feel badly, I say to myself, "Don't be afraid, make a plan, be comforted with prayer and don't be scared to make decisions to change."

Fate has a habit of taking us on paths we don't expect. I thought I would be an interior designer until I retired; however, my illness steered me in another direction. Today, through my consulting business, *Healthy Home, Healthy You, by Maggie*, I educate my clients about what it takes to create a healthy environment for themselves and their loved ones—including their pets. Most importantly, I help them become empowered around their own health and let them know they are not alone.

We live in a time of incredible technological advancements; unfortunately, we also live in a time when dangerous chemicals have invaded every aspect of our lives, causing not only MCS but cancer, asthma, and a host of other diseases. It is my mission to help as many people as possible heal from the effect of these toxins, or, better yet, avoid illness altogether. There is no quick fix; it takes time and commitment, but it's well worth it to be able to join the world again. My motto is "healthy home today…healthy YOU tomorrow"

ABOUT THE AUTHOR: Maggie Poetz is an author, licensed Interior Designer, LEED AP and Certified Green Building Professional. Maggie's journey began with the sudden appearance of debilitating symptoms of "unknown cause." Her search for answers led to building materials and chemicals in her environment; it also ignited a passion to help others. Her company, Healthy Home Healthy You by Maggie, is dedicated to leading the war on environmental toxins and empowering people to regain their health by creating healthy homes. When she is not speaking to groups or assisting clients, she can be found practicing Yoga or on the beach, enjoying the sun and healing properties of the fresh sea air.

Maggie Poetz
Healthy Home Healthy You By Maggie LLC
healthyhomebymaggie.com
Maggie@healthyhomebymaggie.com
561-346-7234

The Power of Pain
Allyson Fusella

In the words of Maya Angelou, "There is no greater agony than bearing the weight of an untold story inside of you." My story begins with my mother, the person I counted on to love and support me unconditionally. I believed this love to be my birthright, a guarantee, never questioning the possibility of its absence. Failing to find the ever-elusive key that would unlock my mother's heart was a pain that cut me so deep, I spent the first half of my life running from it.

Growing up, it was just me and my mother. The situation should have strengthened our relationship, but the exact opposite proved true. My mother gave the best part of herself to the rest of the world. Her never-ending need for adoration, acknowledgement, and recognition always pulled her in a thousand directions, and always away from me. I started to see myself through my mother's eyes, unaware that her inadequacies were all she could see in me. I tried to be enough, I tried to be more than enough, but I could not get there. I did not know how to advocate for my own needs because I never knew I had a right to have them. I learned to push them down, hide them away, and ignore my own voice.

As an adult, I recognized "love" as emotional disengagement, which negatively influenced my choices. At age twenty-four, I chose a marriage that required me to overcome prodigious obstacles. I believed I could only be loved based on my ability to give and meet others' needs, with absolutely no consideration for my own. I thought I had to "earn" love, so I would compromise myself every time. It was all I had ever known. It was what I knew to be love. It was what I learned from my mother.

I fully intended to continue denying, ignoring, burying, and pretending, but the migraines eventually made it impossible to do so. In my twenties they were manageable; I did not know to listen to my pain. In my thirties they were frequent and intense, but my three small children were my priority; I did not have time to listen to my pain. In my forties, they were daily and debilitating; I had no choice but to listen to my pain. Emotional pain is easy to hide but physical pain demands acknowledgement. With every migraine, the intensity got stronger, the knock-down was harder, and it took me longer to get up. The physical pain reverberated down to my very soul, and I knew intuitively that it was there to serve as a mirror to the emotional pain I had locked inside.

I felt alone because I had come to believe that if I did not matter to my own parents, I did not matter, period. This belief lived inside of me, affected my thinking, and filled me with fear. I was aware that the fear was powerful enough to destroy me, but I began to see the potential it held to propel me forward. When I was forty-six, my oldest son turned sixteen, which was the most traumatic year of my childhood. The dichotomy between the pain and trauma of my sixteenth year and the beauty and the joy I was able to create in his life ignited a fury in me that I could no longer contain.

I knew I had to confront my mother, face the terror of inevitable rejection and heal my own soul. My adult mind fiercely resisted this truth, but my heart told a different story. I had to allow my heart to break because the crack is how the light gets in. If I didn't change something, nothing would change, and it had to start with me. I knew I possessed so much love, so much passion, and so much color, but I was watching it all fade to black. Although I felt crushed and broken, deep inside I sensed hope.

I began to search for the roadblocks that were keeping me stuck. Initially, I had to actually be in physical pain to stop running long enough to listen to that still small voice. For me, that was the hardest part. The physical pain forced me to feel. At first, the anger, frustration, betrayal, sadness, loneliness, and disgust were aimed at my migraines, then at my mother, then at me. I recognized I had failed to love myself. I had denied my value, given my power away, and allowed someone else to determine my worth.

I decided to take some time to observe my life. I observed my relationships and how I allowed other people to treat me. I observed without judgment, which lifted the fog of guilt and condemnation. It is amazing how much clarity was possible when I took the time to be still. I wrote in a plain black notebook to release the pieces of me that I was ready to let go. I ripped some pages into small pieces, burned some, crumpled some and threw them all away. It was how I chose to finally acknowledge and honor my pain. Patterns, beliefs, habits, and reactions started to emerge, and the discoveries surprised and amazed me. I uncovered exquisite gems that I recorded in a beautiful journal I resolved to fill with inspiration. This journal held the fragile pieces of my broken heart, so that I could eventually start piecing it back together.

The journey to heal was arduous. Initially, I did not recognize the lessons because they were overshadowed by pain. I did not get to choose what I was to learn, just how many times I wanted to travel around the same mountain before I decided to stop, listen, and pay attention. Awareness is the first step towards change. I could not change what I would not acknowledge. I had to own and accept my story before I could be accountable for the results of my actions and decisions. I learned that I can choose whether a belief, behavior, thought or action is serving me. If it is not, I can choose to let it go. I can choose strength when I feel weak. I can choose courage when I feel afraid. I can choose integrity when I am confused. I can choose to trust my own truth. I can choose to receive the love that surrounds me. I had forgotten how powerful I am.

I choose who I am and who I want to be. My value is not dependent upon another person's ability to see it. I choose to pay attention to the light inside of me and I am determined to shine bright. Self-care and self-love is the ultimate destination, and gratitude is the road that led me there. Discovering my own beauty and magnificence made it impossible not to see it in others. This opened the way to understanding, empathy and forgiveness for those that had failed to see it in me.

Another person's inability to love me only had the power to crush me when I allowed it to define me. When I chose to see it as their burden to bear, with no effect on my worthiness to be loved, it could no longer hurt me. This illuminating truth had the ability to transform my pain, allowing my heart to open to compassion and forgiveness for everyone, including myself. This has served to strengthen my spirit, call me higher, and force me to grow. I discovered it was possible to give myself the unconditional love I desired, but only when I started to believe I was worth it. I am responsible for my own heart. Loving and believing in myself is how I found my way. God used the very boulder that knocked me down as a stepping stone to propel me to unimaginable heights.

I thought my prayers went unanswered because the miracles I received did not appear to be what I was asking or hoping for. I prayed for relief from physical pain. The miracle is that the relentless physical pain served as a bridge to hidden emotional pain I had inadvertently carried inside of me my whole life. The physical pain gave me an even stronger determination to become more than I might have become otherwise. The miracle is that I did not have to be healed to be of service. I recognized that it is in the pain where the greatest gifts lie and the deepest connections are formed. Empathy, compassion, and love are strengthened when bonded through pain.

I prayed to understand what was wrong with me, what had deemed me unlovable. The miracle is that I discovered the power of self-love. In spite of my own difficulties, I was able to soar. I don't have to be perfect to be whole. I learned that I can have problems and still have peace. I still get migraines, but only when I don't take care of myself. I try to see them as a reminder that I am out of balance, rather than use them as an excuse to stop trying to bring the best of myself to every day. I have learned to search for gratitude in the most unlikely places. It is never easy, but it is always worth it.

I prayed to receive the strength, knowledge, and understanding to accomplish goals that would make me good enough. The miracle is that as I began to recognize and embrace the lessons, I discovered that my journey has blessed me with all that and so much more. I have always been good enough. As I chose to heal myself, God taught me to heal others. I have received extraordinary insight and wisdom, and my collective experiences and unique qualifications have enabled me to start a successful business helping others heal from the same pain that could have crushed me. I offer guidance to my clients as they search for the areas of their lives that need to heal to achieve balance of mind, body, and spirit. I encourage hope as my clients navigate their own pain to discover the beauty and the joy and the lessons that are unique to them.

I never dreamed I would have the courage to share my story and allow anyone to see the scars of my broken heart. I never in a million years dreamed that those very scars would be the road map I would use to help others find their way. Sometimes the smallest step in the right direction can end up being the biggest step of your life. The road ahead may be unclear, but take the step. There is one thing I know for sure: wherever my journey takes me, it is exactly where I am meant to be.

ABOUT THE AUTHOR: Allyson Fusella is a Board Certified Holistic Health Coach with the American Association of Drugless Practitioners and the owner of Foundations Nutrition and Wellness Coaching. Her heart-centered wellness program addresses the complex emotional issues that contribute to heart disease, the leading cause of death in the U.S. Allyson's passion is helping her clients reach their individual wellness goals by empowering them to access their own inner wisdom and guidance to make choices that nourish mind, body, and soul.

Allyson Fusella, AADP, CHC
Foundations Nutrition & Wellness Coaching, LLC
foundationscoach.com
Allyson@Foundationscoach.com
973-396-2408

Meditating on the Subway
My Strange, Circuitous Journey to Spirituality
Dana Micheli

I have never been what you would call a patient person. My jaw clenches when a line at the market is unreasonably long, and I regularly swear at some technological device that takes too long to boot up or download. The same is true for activities that are supposed to be relaxing. For many years now, a long walk has been part of my daily routine; it is both exercise and a means of transportation. Rain or shine, I zip around my Brooklyn neighborhood to do grocery shopping and other errands, and inevitably someone gets in my way. It might be one person in front of me, shuffling slowly along, eyes glued to his or phone while sending a text, or three people walking abreast on the sidewalk. I'm not rude to them; I don't shoot them dirty looks or say anything, but I am annoyed as I squeeze past them and dart ahead. Sometimes, I see slow-moving folks and take another block altogether. If wait is a four-letter word in New York, then I am a New Yorker on steroids.

About ten years ago, I attended an event at a rather chichi pre-school where my friend worked. There was a silent auction that included many incredible items and experiences, from a weekend at someone's Hamptons home to one-of-a-kind pieces of jewelry designed by a local artist. At the end of the night, I was very excited to hear that I had won the series of yoga classes at an Upper East Side studio. Now, I knew when I bid on it that it was quite a hike from where I live, but I'd heard of this particular place and decided it was worth it. I needed something to stretch the body, clear the mind, and just unplug. I tried to hang onto this thought as the subway quite literally crawled all the way from my neighborhood (those of you who have experienced the New York City Transit system can attest to the fact that when you need to get somewhere by a certain time, the train or bus is inevitably delayed). By the time I reached the stop and began weaving around the human obstacle course on the street, my mood was anything but zen. I wanted a meaningful experience, dammit, and it seemed the entire world was conspiring against my having it. Even in the moment, I was aware of how ridiculous my attitude was, as well as the fact that this could have been avoided if I had just left my house earlier. I had participated, to some extent, in the creation of this drama.

Why do I mention this? Because even as I was being sucked into the outer turmoil, on the inside I was craving a deeper, more meaningful, spiritual state-of-being. I had always craved it; I just wasn't sure how to get there. I grew up sort-of Catholic, which was to say I was forced to endure (and often skipped) catechism classes and the occasional mass, which I tuned out as they did not resonate with me. Yet I'd always believed in God and had the sense that being close to the Divine was not only possible but closer to our natural state than it outwardly appeared. I once told a friend I felt the presence of God more in a park than in a church, to which he good-naturedly replied, "You're a pagan!" I didn't know what I was; all I knew was that it seemed that achieving oneness required me to go somewhere special. I was also under the impression that this oneness would be achieved instantly, like a being struck by a bolt of lightning. In a way, I was right and wrong on both counts. I would go somewhere special, but it was inward rather than at a yoga studio, and the path would be lit by a series of "lightning bolts."

It began when an equally high-strung friend of mine handed me a CD and described it as life-changing. I saw the words Daily Dose written across it in black Sharpie and raised an eyebrow at her. She told me it was a simple but powerful meditation (actually, she probably said something like, it "helps you forget about crap for a while," which sounded just fine to me). A few days later, I popped in the CD and rolled out the yoga mat, not at all sure what to expect. As the soft female voice guided me in progressive muscle relaxation, my mind immediately began to race. Was I wasting my time with this? Would I be good at it? The more she suggested I stop thinking, the more I felt it wasn't working. But I continued to lay there and focus on my desire to connect. Suddenly, I was filled with this incredible feeling of peace. For the first time in years, maybe even decades, I had a sense of the "me" that observed all the surface drama without buying into or being affected by it. The feeling, I realized, could only be described as a homecoming, and when I felt it I burst into tears. I had just connected with my own soul, and in doing so, had been struck by what would be the first of many spiritual lightning bolts.

That experience taught me once and for all that I do not have to go to a special class in order to connect with the Divine. I did the Daily Dose for a while, but never had such a profound experience again, in part because after a few times I memorized the words and anticipated them, which was distracting. I had never used YouTube before, but now I found myself searching through literally hundreds of meditations. It took a while for me to find the ones that most resonated with me, but each time I did, it brought me on a new profound inner adventure. Some days I felt myself leaving my body and travelling in nature; other times I would go to some city or town I had never been before, surrounded by faces I didn't know yet were eerily familiar. Whatever happened, I felt a joy and connectedness I had never experienced before, and anything that had been bothering me beforehand seemed completely irrelevant and, most importantly, something I could banish from my life.

One day I saw the face of my great-aunt who had passed away when I was ten. She was smiling happily, as she so often did in life. I came out of meditation a bit startled. Why had I seen Aunt Jo? She had been a wonderful woman and the heart of my extended family, but other than my parents' stories I barely remembered her. She was definitely not on my mind on a regular basis. The next day, my mother called to tell me that her husband, my Uncle Steve, had passed away. It wasn't until we hung up the phone that I remembered seeing Jo. Was she telling me that she was waiting for him? I hesitated before telling his daughter. First, I didn't want to upset her further, and second, I was afraid she might think I was nuts. Instead, she said, "Oh my God! Shortly after Dad passed I walked into his bedroom and actually saw my mother standing over him!" In the sharing of the story, we had both received validation for what we had seen and felt.

After meditating every day for a few months, I began to see a shift in my waking moments as well. While walking around the city I no longer just saw concrete and hordes of people, but the many trees and beautiful flowers planted and lovingly tended to by the people who live there. Above the din of honking horns and blasting car radios I heard the busy chirping of birds. Even a subway ride became a place to close my eyes and instantly be transported into a more relaxed state. My outward reality had not changed all that much, yet I found myself wanting for absolutely nothing. I was what New Agers commonly refer to as "blissed out."

Many other things happened during this time that lent credence to my journey. For example, I just "happened" to meet a woman on Facebook whose writing and editing business catered largely to psychics, Reiki masters, lightworkers, and others across the spiritual spectrum. I began working with her and through our clients began learning about the path of the seeker and how my frustrated attempts at getting on this path had caused much of the angst in my life. I became aware of my many limiting beliefs and the extent to which my present was controlled by my perceptions of the past. Apparently, while I had been rushing around and working like a dog to make life happen, I had also been subconsciously manifesting a spiritual path.

I don't know when it started, but one day I noticed that my experiences in meditation had become less and less dramatic. The sense of euphoria was gone, as was the feeling of profound connectedness. I didn't doubt the validity of what I had seen and felt, I just couldn't seem to get back to that place. Feeling lost and forsaken, I turned to Google and began trying to figure out what was happening. I wasn't alone, of course; in fact, I found what I was going through was quite common. Spiritual progress, it seemed, was like everything else in life—it ebbs and flows. It is easy enough to believe when you feel energy shooting up your spine or realize that the painful event from twenty years ago has no power over you anymore; it is much harder to follow a spiritual path when you feel like you can no longer "escape" reality through meditation. Change of this significance requires faith, and a great deal of patience. I also learned that when meditation stops being so dramatic, it means we are integrating what we have learned into our everyday lives. These days I continue to have many aha moments, and even now and again a lightning bolt. The difference is that when things are quiet, I have faith that I will connect again and in a more evolved manner. I also know I am being taught the value of waiting for things in Divine order, not my own.

I am still not the most patient person, at least not when it comes to the day-to-day business of life. I still rush around the neighborhood, and I still get annoyed when something takes too long to download a file on the computer. But I have become much more patient when it comes to the bigger things in life. I have also realized that even the most reluctant, irreverent meditators can connect with the world beyond texts, transit, and linear time.

ABOUT THE AUTHOR: Dana Micheli is a ghostwriter, editor, and owner of Writers in the Sky Creative Writing Services. She has ghostwritten and edited nonfiction and fiction books across several genres, including spirituality; business and legal matters; science fiction/fantasy; romance and crime. Before pursuing her writing career full-time, Dana served as a lobbyist on behalf of the Arizona Coalition Against Domestic Violence and as the Manager of PR/Communications for The New York Women's Foundation. She has also worked for several media outlets, writing and researching legal, political and human interest stories for print, online and television. Dana has a B.A. in English from Southern Connecticut University and a Juris Doctor from New York Law School. She lives in Brooklyn, New York.

Dana Micheli
writersinthesky.com
dana@writersinthesky.com
646-504-3615
facebook.com/dana.micheli

When the Student is Ready
Kathy Fyler

It all started with a "neon emergency."

A "big" client that we had been trying to land for several months called in a frenzy because they were having a promotion and their current manufacturer pulled out at the last minute. Bottom line: they needed one hundred signs within forty-eight hours.

"How can we make a hundred neon signs in two days?" I said to Sue, my partner. "It's nearly impossible."

Always the optimist, Sue replied, "We may not be able to do actual neon signs, but we can definitely make a hundred Better Than Neon™ signs. It's still a stretch, and I think we can do it!"

We had started our sign and display company in 1994 and after six years we were still struggling. In order to open more doors and attract more clients we had obtained a patent for a sign design that we created. It was a lighted sign that looked like neon, but wasn't as labor intensive and costly as an actual neon sign. This would be perfect for our client.

At the time I had been studying the words of thought leader Napoleon Hill. In his book *Keys to Success: The 17 Principles of Personal Achievement,* Hill had talked about "going the extra mile," which he defined as giving more service and goods than expected. This, he said, would put you in the good graces of your customer and anyone else you apply this principle to.

For the next forty-eight hours we put all our resources and energy into this one order and were able to produce and deliver the hundred signs to our client! In time, we would find out how important "going the extra mile" was.

Breakthrough

My personal development journey started when I was gifted "Personal Power" by Tony Robbins. It was a set of fifteen cassette tapes (remember those?!) with a lesson for each day on one side. It took thirty days to complete the set if you were vigilant and did the lessons daily. Sue was excited to "play along" so after all the employees left for the day, we'd sit in the large, open, attic office of our manufacturing building and pop a cassette into the player.

There were great lessons that invited us to delve into "self." One of the most eye-opening exercises was about evaluating where you currently were in your life and then visualizing what life would be like if you didn't make any changes. WOW, it was powerful. At the time money was tight—so tight that I remember paying the delivery man for our Chinese food with rolled pennies I had been saving. To think what my life would be like in one, five, and ten years if I remained on the same track was very painful indeed. As we listened to the tapes, Sue and I realized we needed to make some serious changes.

We sat down to have a serious meeting about the direction and intention of our business. We looked over our sales, customers, prospects, employees, cash flow, production—all of it. We re-committed ourselves to the business and made decisions and plans to get us on a positive trajectory. The biggest decision was to hire a production manager with specialized experience—and even though it would cost us $70k, we knew in our hearts that it was worth it and would help us reach our goals.

In 1999, we learned that Tony Robbins was going to host an event called Results 2000 at the Meadowlands Arena in New Jersey, not far from where we lived. There would be several famous people speaking there—Barbara Walters, Christopher Reeves, Brian Tracy, and General Norman Schwarzkopf, to name a few. Sue and I were excited to see Tony Robbins live because of the changes we'd made as a result of listening to his cassette program. So we both took the day off (an unusual occurrence) and headed over to the arena.

While at Results 2000 an amazing thing happened. Remember that client that we went "the extra mile" for? Well they called and awarded us with a *million-dollar* order! We hadn't come close to that amount in one year, let alone one order. Sue and I cried with joy!

Someone also handed us free tickets to a Tony Robbins "Breakthrough," all-day session. Even though it was on a Saturday, I decided to work that weekend instead because we were super busy with our million-dollar order, so Sue went for the both of us.

That evening, she returned from Breakthrough filled with energy and excitement.

"It was such a great event that I signed us up for two all-weekend events!" she announced.

"Awesome, I can't wait," I replied. "Are they free too?"

"Well, not exactly."

"How much is 'not exactly'?" I questioned.

"Five thousand dollars."

When the momentary shock passed, I knew she had made the right decision. At the time five thousand dollars was a huge stretch for us; on the other hand, the small amount of money that I had spent on my personal development thus far had already paid dividends.

Sure enough, Tony Robbins' weekend events, "Unleash the Power Within" and "Personal Power II" were amazing and worth more than we paid. What a great way to immerse myself into personal development and self-improvement. What I learned most from the events was that in order to be successful, it was important to continue working on myself and to surround myself with like-minded people.

Beyond Personal Power

I left the events wanting more and, as the saying goes, "When the student is ready, the teacher appears." For me, Marianne Williamson was the next to show up. I purchased Marianne's book, *A Return to Love,* and fell in love with her teachings. The book taught me to act and live from my heart space. To live from love, not fear or ego. This shifted my quest from personal growth to spiritual growth.

Next, a friend suggested another great book, Thomas L. Pauley's

I'm Rich Beyond My Wildest Dreams--I Am. I Am. I Am. This was my introduction to manifesting my dreams and desires. Yes, I had been writing down my goals, but this book showed me that I could create my reality with my thoughts and intentions.

Pauley's method was simple. Buy a spiral notebook and on the first page write, "All this by Divine Right. Divine Inspiration, Divine Intervention, Divine Timing and with Good for all concerned." Find something that you desire in your life and then write it down as if you already have this thing. Next, close your eyes and imagine it with all your senses, then write them down. At the time I was looking to buy a home, so I did the exercise and wrote down everything I wanted in a home—from the outside to every detail inside. The last thing on the list was always "it is easily paid for". Then you let the Universe do the rest.

One Sunday I set out looking for homes. I had my list with all the open houses and visited many of them, but none seemed to resonate with me. Just as I was about to call it a day, I was guided to take a couple of turns. I went with the feeling, and as I rounded a corner, there was a sign for an open house that wasn't on my list. I decided to check it out. As I got out of the car, I saw that the condo was not an end unit–something that was really important to me. I almost got back into my car, but I felt an urging to see the condo anyway. The house was wonderful and because of the wall of windows along the whole back wall, it didn't feel like a middle unit. Almost all of the things that I asked the Universe for were in this home… and in less than a few months the condo was mine!

Several years later, when I moved from this home, I rented a home in Cape May, New Jersey. Amazingly, this home was much more like the house I had *originally* described in my spiral notebook. The Universe was still looking out for me!

Powerful You! was manifested using the same principles. For years, one of my major intentions was to help women entrepreneurs. Today, our Powerful You! Women's Network helps women to connect with other women and provide support and resources to female entrepreneurs and all women. And because Sue and I had experienced and know the value of personal and spiritual growth, we were able to incorporate it into the heart of our business.

Teachers are Everywhere

My teachers continued to show up when I needed them. Three women we met through our network and became friends with— Jennifer, Donna, and Laura—were teaching a course based on The Seven Spiritual Laws of Success by Deepak Chopra. These lessons made a profound shift for me because they gave me even more tools to create my life as I wanted it to be. These "laws" opened my eyes to the amazing gifts of the Universe, and helped me know that everything happens for a reason, and for my highest and best good, even if it doesn't feel like it at the time. For example, if we had not lost our manufacturing business—which felt devastating at the time—we wouldn't have attended a networking luncheon, and the seeds for Powerful You! might not have been planted.

For most people their parents are their first teachers and I have learned much from mine. I learned from observing my parents' relationship to love unconditionally and to respect a partner's individuality. I also learned that what some people might call compromise is better described as honoring the desires of another person and gratefully doing what it takes to make them happy. Mom and Dad continue to do this even after fifty-nine years of marriage.

Sometimes our greatest teachers are the ones that are right in front of us. Sue Urda, my partner of twenty-four years, has been my most important teacher, and her wisdom has influenced my life is so many ways. Most importantly, she has taught me to live my life from the heart and recognize the "feel good" in every moment. One of the earliest "lessons" was to truly enjoy food as I was eating it— something I didn't even know I was missing out on. Whether we are watching a movie, laughing at silly jokes, walking on the beach and watching the dolphins, or practicing our daily rituals, she reminds me to enjoy the process and focus on what's good about what's around us.

Over the course of my journey I've become increasingly aware that there are many teachers in my midst, and that they'll show up exactly when I need them. Life is full of wondrous lessons and experiences and I am grateful to be on this path of openness and expansion. As I contemplate my years of spiritual growth I have been blessed with incredible teachers, rich life experiences with people I love, and life lessons that serve me. It is my sincere hope and intention that I am a teacher for others too.

ABOUT THE AUTHOR: Kathy's earlier career includes being a Critical Care Nurse, Project Manager for a technology firm, and owner of a $5 million manufacturing company. In 2005, Kathy followed her calling to make "more of a contribution to what matters most in this world". Using her experience and passion for technology and people, she co-founded Powerful You! Women's Network and Powerful You! Publishing to fulfill her personal mission of assisting women in creating connections via the internet, live meetings and the published word. Kathy is an Amazon #1 Bestselling Author who loves to travel the country connecting with and teaching women.

Kathy Fyler
Co-Founder of Powerful You! Inc.
powerfulyou.com
powerfulyoupublishing.com
info@powerfulyou.com

The A, B and Cs of Caring for the Elderly

A Road Map from Personal Experience
Terri-Sue Hill

We've all heard the saying, "Old habits die hard." Well, as a retired schoolteacher, I was accustomed to planning ahead. Unfortunately, nothing could have prepared me for the dynamics involved in caring for a loved one with dementia. In this case, the loved one is my mother, someone who has been my rock and my inspiration for as long as I can remember. Now however, it is my turn to take the reins. It is my turn to be the blanket of safety, comfort, and encouragement that she was for me.

How can I begin to advise others how to cope, when I am in a continuous state of reformation? I am re-forming the manner in which I carry out my daily routines, which have now become *our* daily routines. I constantly tell myself that I must be flexible. I must learn to just "roll with it" and let things flow and unfold in their own way.

At some point in this process of trial and error, I began keeping a journal. It was nothing formal at first; I just found myself typing my thoughts and frustrations while I worked on other self-imposed assignments. It was my way of venting, allowing myself to review events, and make positive choices moving forward. I found that the more I thought things through, the more I would recall other moments that brought me clarity and gave me a greater perspective on how to handle our new living and learning conditions.

Eventually, in addition to my computer journal, I began keeping a little book by my bed. I made notes of things that went well and things that had not and placed an X next to them. As I became more organized (remember, ex-teacher, old habits), I began putting my thoughts in alphabetical order so I could easily retrieve and refer back to them. Below are my "A, B, Cs" of dealing with dementia. It is a work in progress, but it is my sincere hope that you will be able to use my experiences as reference points on your own journey.

A ~

Anxiety is a key factor when dealing with dementia, for both the sufferer and the caretaker. It was one of the first emotions my mother identified in the days leading up to her diagnosis. She had this constant feeling of impending doom. She felt the need to keep everything closed, with windows shut and curtains drawn so that no one could look in the house. She wanted to go out, yet she was hesitant about it, which made her very depressed. I became anxious as well. I wanted to do something to lift her spirits, something that would help her to regain the positive attitude she once had for life.

Aromatherapy and Essential oils can be extremely helpful in easing the symptoms of dementia. Our olfactory nerves both create and evoke memories—pleasant or unpleasant. The smell of cookies can remind you of your grandmother's kitchen, or the lunch lady who was mean to you at school. Therefore, before using aromatherapy with your loved one, you must carefully consider the objectives you wish to achieve (i.e. create a state of rest and relaxation).

Oftentimes people with dementia or Alzheimer's have trouble sleeping. This can be unhealthy for them as well as their caregivers. Many people, including my mother, find lavender helpful for relaxation. However, it may have a different effect on someone who associates it with sadness or melancholy. In that case, you might try Melissa essential oil, or perhaps Chamomile. If you want them to feel more awake and energetic, you might try peppermint or a citrus blend of some sort. It's up to you and your loved one to decide what's best.

Once you choose your oils, you can then decide whether you want to use them in the room where your loved one spends most of his/her time or have the fragrance wafting throughout the house (diffusers work well in either regard). Always check with doctors and pharmacists before using oils, as some may not be compatible with certain medications.

Affirmations are a good tool to use when loved ones become discouraged over an inability to do the things they once found so easy. Practice using them on a regular basis. Here are some of my mother's favorites.

I am happy, healthy, whole and healed in mind, body, and spirit.
I am blessed, healed, and strengthened by the power and the glory of God.
I can do all things through Christ who strengthens me.

B ~

Balanced lives are essential to the survival of everyone involved. This means that in order to be of service to my mother, I must also take care of my own personal and medical needs.

Whenever possible, I try to schedule our doctors' appointments so that the calendar is more manageable. I also constantly remind myself to take time for self-maintenance. Something as simple as taking a walk can feel like a mini vacation when you feel overwhelmed with responsibilities. Learn to ask for help—you know a friend, neighbor, or relative close by. Don't be shy about asking for a few minutes of their time.

The Alzheimer's Association can also be of help. I have called several times when faced with a situation I didn't know how to remedy. They were very understanding, offered suggestions, and even followed up with a call to see how I was coping.

Body Clock Adjustments (*yours and theirs*) - After my mother was diagnosed with dementia, I realized that major adjustments had to be made to our daily routine so that Mom's eating, sleeping, and medications could be managed. Maintaining proper nutrition is an essential part of caring for someone with this issue; it's also important to keep the caregiver's strength up. Try to plan meals that will serve all family members' needs. That way, you will save both time and money.

A good night's rest is invaluable. If possible, make sure the televisions are off by a certain time each night, as this will reduce noise and create a relaxed atmosphere. Try listening to soft music, drawing or painting, or reading and writing. This is what we do in our home, and I've found it helps everyone have a more restful night.

C ~

Calendar - Post a calendar that is large enough for your loved one to see. Celebrate successes along the way. This will help you to chronicle his/her progress and observe trends in behavior and diet. I purchased a lightweight, whiteboard calendar and markers and placed it on Mom's closet door. I record all of her appointments and whether or not she walked that day. Each morning I cross out the previous day so that she is able to keep track of what day it is. Sometimes she remembers and sometimes she doesn't, but this provides an extra reminder.

Clothing should be easy to put on and take off, allowing for changes in fine motor skills. They should open in the front, with buttons, zippers or Velcro, or be able to be pulled over the head.

Place the clothing on the bed as an incentive to get dressed for the day. Even if they choose something else, at least they are thinking and making choices; maintaining self-empowerment. Ultimately, it should be whatever works for them.

Cognition and Communication - Communicate with your loved one even though he/she may not remember.

When my mother was diagnosed with dementia, there were several other things going on in her body, including hemorrhoids, diverticulitis and irritable bowel syndrome. She was unable to differentiate these painful conditions from one another, so the doctors and I had to be patient when trying to find out what was wrong.

Comprehending and processing information is very difficult for my mother. Even when she thinks she understands, the facts become jumbled in her mind and she cannot articulate those parts that she cannot comprehend. You will find yourself repeating the same information so often that you question your own ability to make yourself clear. This is where patience and understanding become challenging on both ends. I find myself referring to my teacher training and focusing on various learning modalities when trying to get my mother to understand the information she needs or wants to know. Sometimes using a combination of kinesthetic, visual or tactile means of communication works best.

Childproofing your home - Senior-proofing can be very similar. My mother is very zealous about maintaining her independence; however, there are several daily tasks she is no longer able to accomplish. I have to supervise just about everything to make sure she does not do something detrimental to her health and safety.

The kitchen is particularly dangerous; she might leave the stove on, potentially causing a fire or gas leak. Our refrigerator has a bell that rings if it is left open; however, my mother is hard of hearing, so it is of little use to her. Someone has to be with her at all times.

The bathroom is another challenging area. Mom needs help getting into and out of the bathtub, even when she thinks she can do it on her own. I've found that placing some sort of adhesive traction on the bottom and sides of the tub are helpful. Handles can also be a valuable resource. Of course there are walk-in tubs (which can be quite costly), and shower chairs.

If your loved one has difficulty standing and sitting, you may need to think about raising the toilet seat. There are special ones that fit right on top of the regular seat, and some even have handles so the person can brace him or herself.

Electrical sockets are another concern. My mother has a nightlight and a motion detector in her bathroom, both of which are helpful. The nightlight helps her get to the bathroom, and the motion detector gives her a little more light once she gets there. The main overhead light is too bright for her to leave on in the middle of the night.

Cross-reference all the useful information you gather along the way and look for common threads. Then compile it and keep it handy so you are not constantly trying to reinvent the wheel. Know that there will be changes and adjustments along the way. Try to maintain as much consistency as you can so that you don't lose sight of your main objectives, namely, to do what is in the best interest of your loved one while trying to preserve your own health and well-being. Remember, you are not alone and there are resources out there for you.

These tips from my personal experience have helped me to navigate the tricky waters as I care for my mom, and I'm learning new things every day. Sometimes it feels confusing like alphabet soup and other times it feels happy and organized like the alphabet song. I am committed to creating a flow that will make it a little easier to alphabetically navigate your way through this difficult journey and discern the best path for you and your loved one.

ABOUT THE AUTHOR: Terri-Sue Hill is a writer, certified life coach, and voiceover artist. She authored two children's books, both of which received the Family Choice Award, and is a member of the Society of Children's Book Writers and Illustrators. Her past experience includes over twenty-five years as a teacher and two years as host of the VoiceAmerica Internet Radio Talk Show, *Frame of Mind.* She is a licensed Heal Your Life workshop leader. In addition, she uses art and writing to help people use their inner voices to discover their hidden passions. Her favorite pastimes include nature and listening to jazz.

Terri-Sue Hill
terri.suehill@yahoo.com

Recalibrated:
My Perfectly Vegan Life
Ananda "Bliss" Kenboya

Full Circle.

I had found it, the missing piece! Packed away in the garage, in an unassuming crate filled with outdated papers from the 1990s, *it* consisted of several handouts and a handwritten summary of a discussion long ago. The worn pages were from a time in my life when I did not understand the words or the messages they held; now, nearly twenty years later, the discussion captured in blue curly scribble was the final piece of a puzzle that brought to life a picture of radiant, vibrant health.

The summary contained sage wisdom from Jennifer, a holistic practitioner who had performed an Iridology inspection of my eyes in order to determine the health of my physical body. During the consultation additional insights were provided regarding my spiritual body. As I listened eagerly she shared information that spelled out my destiny: illness based on how I was living. She also offered an antidote—a way I could set a new course in motion by designing and implementing a solid health and spiritual regimen. I didn't say anything, but I am certain the look on my face told her what I was thinking: "I have no idea what you are talking about!" After all, how could this total stranger look at my eyes and know anything about my future? Aside from being a little chubby, I was perfectly healthy! My blood pressure was good and my doctor never mentioned any issues with my kidneys or liver or any fibroids— whatever *those* were…

Despite my obvious doubts, Jennifer pressed on, sharing more about my spiritual world than I was ready for. She seemed to see right inside of me and know the longings, disappointments and past hurts. How could she know these things about me? Perhaps the eyes really were the window to the soul! Some of the things she suggested—like changing my eating habits and increasing my exercise—made sense to me, as did developing a meditation practice, which I had already begun the previous year. The other activities, however, such as Yoga and Tai Chi, I knew nothing about. I *certainly* did not see myself as a dancer, teacher, painter, singer, actor, or writer! Yet Jennifer was gentle but confident when she stated that my current trajectory would lead me to poor physical health and a less than blissful life.

As the session came to an end, Jennifer suggested I keep her notes and handouts for a future time when I would be able to understand them and embrace the message. I agreed and went on my way, feeling more than a little skeptical. Unbeknownst me, however, a seed had been planted and my life was about to change. The "scavenger hunt" had already begun. Even so, it would be another twenty years before I understood how all the experiences, including this one, were the very pieces of the puzzle bringing into focus the beauty and bliss that is my life now.

What's up with my blood pressure?

Why was my foot swollen? I did not remember falling down or hurting myself, there was no bruising and my foot did not hurt, so why was it swollen? Finally, after thirty days I went to see my doctor and was given the news that I was pre-hypertensive. It came as no surprise that I "fit the profile" for hypertension: I was nearing my fortieth birthday, was overweight (at barely five-foot-three I was closing in on two hundred pounds), a stressed-out single mom with money issues, and a Black American. I was given a daily water pill and soon my foot was back to normal. On my next visit to the doctor's office I was given a refill and told it was, "highly unlikely that I would ever be rid of the pills" and "I should expect my blood pressure to continue to climb" and to "only be controlled by medication." I left feeling defeated and dissatisfied with this outlook, and I wondered how my "birthright" could be circumvented.

During my meditation time I began to focus my intention on healing the part of me that seemed in alignment with hypertension. I soon remembered a book given to me by a friend: Louise L. Hay's *You Can Heal Your Life*. I had never read it, but now it seemed to beckon me as if it knew I was ready to receive its message. In the back of the book was a section that identified a list of health-related problems, each with a probable cause and a new thought pattern to use as a mantra. As I read about hypertension's probable cause (longstanding unresolved emotional problems), I realized it rang true for me. I began to write, see a therapist and use the mantra as a tool to support my healing. My blood pressure did not continue to climb as my doctor had predicted, yet it was still holding steady at pre-hypertensive. This experience brought the puzzle piece of release and spiritual practice. I was healing my past. Thankful for the new understanding and stabilization of my blood pressure, I knew that there was indeed more work for me to do.

A whisper, a nudge and a ROAR!!!

Equipped with this new information and revelation, I felt unstoppable! Still, questions remained. Why was my blood pressure not going down? Why was my weight going up? Now that I was open spiritually, people and situations showed up in my life to guide me to the next level of understanding. I was now coming in contact with holistic health practitioners and involved in wellness conversations, but while it all seemed familiar to me I did not yet connect it to the session with Jennifer. Eventually, I was led to another book, *Reversing Hypertension* by Julian Whitaker, M.D. This book supported my desire to heal my body of pre-hypertension and rid my life of medication dependency.

I began meditating even more during this time; I jotted down the gentle messages I received while in meditation and contemplated them, hoping to glean some understanding and direction. As I sat with these new puzzle pieces that did not fit together, the Universe provided some prodding in the form of what I now call "health opportunities." My weight was climbing and my face, hands, and feet were puffy. I had terrible monthly cycles that made me moody and achy and I had low energy. I had a gall bladder attack as well.

None of these things were life-threatening, but they were certainly enough to get my attention.

I had rid myself of the old doctor who lacked vision and had found a wonderful, new doctor with whom I could discuss my ideas. It was validating to be aligned with a sane person from the medical community. We would work together to develop a plan of how to get my health to a great place! She reviewed my blood work—including my kidney and liver function—and was very surprised at the findings. On paper, my health looked great, which seemed to directly contradict my appearance and symptoms. My doctor concluded that my symptoms—the gall bladder, terrible cycles, puffiness, low energy and pre-hypertension—were all connected to my weight and my eating/exercise practices.

I was prepared to take her instruction to heart… at least, I thought I was, until she said the unfathomable: "You are morbidly obese." The words lingered, stuck in the air thick and heavy like the stench of popcorn burnt from being overcooked in a microwave. Before I could gather my composure, a BMI chart appeared, seemingly out of thin air. The doctor took her black permanent marker and slowly circled where I fell on the graph. Indeed, it was the area indicating that I was morbidly obese, but that didn't mean I had to believe it. After all, what did this doctor really know about me? Didn't she know Black people weigh more than folks who are not of African descent? Didn't she know the weight charts were created in the 1940s and not relevant now? I stopped listening to the conversation and decided I would experience optimal vibrant health without her help.

I decided to explore ways to heal myself without the assistance of a medical doctor. I took supplements and drank teas that would reduce my blood pressure, cramps, irritability, and dissolve gall stones. It all seemed to work for a while.

Apparently, I was ready to graduate to the next level, because this time the "health opportunities" came roaring into my life like a clap of thunder. I had three surgeries in less than two years. As the symptoms, now severe and sometimes debilitating, continued to multiply I surrendered to the process of surgery. Once healed from the collective procedures I was once again face to face with my weight and the impact it had on my health and quality of life.

Balance was missing during this time. The plan for my life was not one of extremes. Western medical technology could work with holistic practices to experience vibrant health. This was a tough and painful teaching.

The incredible shrinking woman—not! Ever-expanding in consciousness.

Now came the really tough part—I had to get serious about weight loss. I tried diet and exercise programs—too many to even remember them all. I hired fitness trainers, joined walking groups and the gym (multiple times), videos, blogs, new recipes, eating before 7PM, meal replacements, supplements, shakes, drops, appetite suppressants, all-liquid diets, no carbs, no sugar, no flour, no dairy, no gluten, all protein, all citrus, no citrus, more mini meals, skipping meals, and on and on. Some of the plans/programs worked and I lost small amounts of weight. Over time I would gain it back and then some. I had become the typical yo-yo dieter, and a highly perplexed one at that. Despite all I had learned throughout my journey, I remained trapped in a body that did not look like my picture of vibrant health.

What was the lesson for me to know now? There had to be a purpose for what I had gone through and was continuing to go through. In my meditation practice I received a clear message, "in all things be grateful." For me it was easy to have gratitude for all the things that were going well, so I decided to make a list of things in my life I was not very happy with and find something good in it. I contemplated all the diets and exercise plans that I had attempted and what I had learned about myself in that process.

The journey had taught me many things. I learned to recognize when my body was full (the message of cleaning my plate because others were starving no longer resonated with me). I learned an exclusively liquid diet was not a good choice for me; I prefer the intentional practice of enjoying the sight, texture, and flavor of my food, as it was a practice of gratitude for me. I experienced a sense of beauty and connection to others when I shopped for the food. I learned I love vegetables, beans, lentils, and grains, which was a new realization. I learned I was an outlier for my family and I was setting a new course in motion and that our lineage would be forever changed by what I was doing. I learned I did not need meat with every meal or any meal, for that matter. I learned dairy had an effect on my body that I did not like. I learned how much I loved water and the tasty flavors of herbs instead of salt. I learned that my new way of cooking was not only an expression of love and nourishment, it was an art form. I was no longer fixated on my weight; my focus had become the quality and intention of my life.

This gratitude reflection revealed something as surprising as it was incredible: I had largely been practicing a Vegan lifestyle! In fact, I was already 80% plant based. It was not that much of a stretch to decide to go the rest of the way.

Living my life perfectly!

Finding Jennifer's notes and handouts confirmed that every twist and turn down a winding and sometimes dark path was a necessary part of the journey. Her message, filled with symbols and benchmarks, was given to me before I was ready to hear or understand it. That forgotten crate in the garage confirmed it all had to happen the way that it did for my understanding and liberation of choosing a plant-based diet. The pieces all fit together: releasing the past, finding the right helpers/teachers, studying, understanding the messages, being in balance, and the gift of gratitude. This was the content of my spiritual practice, which in turn had given birth to my health regimen. For me the journey to becoming vegan was years in the making. It required moving through a variety of concepts and experiences to embrace where I am now and to live it with ease. There are as many paths to becoming vegan as there are people. This path is uniquely mine. It is conscious, intentional, and balanced. It is perfect.

ABOUT THE AUTHOR: Ananda "Bliss" Kenboya is a masterful storyteller, workshop leader, meditation facilitator, licensed spiritual practitioner, and a certified professional coach. Bliss holds a Master of Human Relations and has more than fifteen years experience working with clients to release limiting beliefs and remove blocks. Through personal experience and recalibration she has developed her intuitive nature and empowers her clients to live their optimal life by consciously designing it. She speaks from the heart, blending her gift of storytelling with a no-nonsense and compassionate approach that inspires others. Bliss is the mother of three adult children and lives in Oakland with her husband Nelson and cat Lola.

Ananda "Bliss" Kenboya MHR, RScP, ELI-MP, CPC
NFocus Coaching
nfocuscoaching.com
nfocuscoaching@gmail.com
Twitter: @coach_ananda

A Spoon Full of Play
Christina Dietz

Following my intuition was easy for the first two decades of my life. I based decisions on my feelings and gut instincts without hesitation. I knew exactly what I wanted to eat for breakfast—my dad's grape jelly and salami sandwiches—and did exactly what I loved to do: create art, go on adventures, and play in nature. But then the Big Love decided to give me a bigger adventure to evolve my intuition: a mysterious illness that would go undiagnosed for four years. It would turn out to be a gift and a golden opportunity to use my heart as a compass.

After my sophomore year at the University of Southern California, I started getting sick on and off and discovered that a really clean diet and exercise (with lots of sweating) kept my mystery infection under control. But after enduring eight months of an undiagnosed parasitic infection from Kenya, a good diet and exercise were no longer enough. I was shocked to see how many "top-notch" doctors from John Hopkins were quick to spit out vague diagnoses because they were simply too embarrassed to admit they didn't know. I was told I had "food allergies," a "weak gut," and a "sensitive personality" and should consider therapy and depression medication. Four years later, I would finally be diagnosed with mycotoxic poisoning—also known as black mold—coupled with arsenic poisoning.

Due to the chronic fungal infection, my senses and vital body parts like my stomach and head were barely working. That's when my Spirit stepped in, guiding me to further develop my intuition to make up for my congested eyes, ears, nose, third eye, and "gut feeling." I was exhausted, couldn't eat, couldn't poop, and felt out of my body, and no one could figure out why. I started coming down with systemic immune-related viruses like mono, shingles, a serious strain of staph, and eventually became celiac.

Infamously known for being nearly impossible to diagnose, black mold severely affects your stomach. Because it was in my intestines, I developed reoccurring parasitic infections and countless food allergies. I could neither digest food nor absorb the nutrients, putting me at fifteen pounds under my normal weight. Every time I ate food, my energy was zapped. Oftentimes, I was done for the day by 11 a.m.—I called these my "horizontal days." Certain types of black mold, including the kind I had, can cross the blood-brain barrier and this is where the condition becomes bizarre and scary.

I developed severe brain fog that felt like an extreme pressure and inflammation in my head, leaving me chronically lightheaded and causing periodic anxiety. Brain-fog, or what felt like cobwebs thickly and tightly wrapped around my brain, caused me to have tunnel vision, feel disoriented, forget where I parked, forget more sophisticated words and forget my foreign languages. Neurotoxicity caused my head to have a poisoned, noxious feeling. I felt like I was adrift in some faraway land, alone and far from help. Many indigenous cultures all over the world agree that the longest journey in life is eighteen inches—from the head to the heart. I didn't have the option of using my head anymore, so I was forced to navigate only from my heart. In fact, my life depended on it.

Intuition, also known as the sixth sense, is what connects us to our Light or higher self. Intuition provides us with a map of sacred, one-of-a kind, music notes that unlock the melodies of our soul's purpose or dreams. Intuition also serves as an internal compass, effortlessly guiding us towards genuine soul growth. In his book *The Resilience of the Heart*, Greg Braden discusses the scientific proof that the heart has its own "brain" that feels and senses independently of the cranial brain. The intuitive heart is even more accurate than the cranial brain because it is without ego. The human experience calls for the heart-brain and cranial brain to work together, with the authentic spirit serving as the guide for the earthly adventure. First, the heart-brain can be used as an instruction manual and compass and then the cranial brain can be used to ground intuition into reality by setting the heart's Divine whispers in motion. Intuition sends serendipitous opportunities and lessons to evolve our soul's understanding of the core of the human experience: unconditional love. In order to receive my never-ending supply of unconditional love, I first had to improve upon *receiving* my intuitive messages.

I had no idea why I was sick and conventional medicine didn't either, so this meant I simply needed to get a little more creative with my approach. First, I got out of my own way and let the Divine blaze my trail. I dropped all resistance to the insecurity in not knowing why I was sick. Dropping all resistance and becoming friendly with your version of uncertainty can put you in a very vulnerable, yet powerful, receiving Yin state for your intuitive messages.

Practicing the passive art of receiving can be challenging in the American culture, which is considered more Yang or masculine-oriented in actively doing and going non-stop. By giving up my ego control for an "answer," I created an open channel to receive any direction I needed in order to navigate my illness. Receiving reaffirms that you are worthy; it also builds up the confidence to say no. I refused to take any anxiety and depression meds suggested to me because I *knew* that they would cloud up the only clear sense I had left: my mama-bear instinct of intuition. Being in receiving mode puts you in total trust in a higher power, where you no longer demand rationality; as a result, ego shrinks and intuition increases.

This trust in Divine delivery freed me to practice the art of zero questioning when it came to my heart-brain's guidance. Since college, I have made every big decision by turning inward and listening to my intuition's repetitive request to ride out my illness by choosing to ride the Light instead. Using my heart compass for guidance, I kept my heart-brain healthy and sharp by consistently turning over every glorious lily pad before me. Then, my intuition spoke to me like it never had before—for months, clearly repeating the same mantra. That mantra was: *New Zealand is the path to wellness.* So, I quit my job at TOMS Shoes and went to hike my dream hike, the Milford Sound, solo. Soon, my illness transformed into an extraordinary adventure outside myself that was completely given up to a Higher Power. I've never felt so taken care of in my life, so much in fact that I almost forgot I was sick. Going to New Zealand allowed me to set a precedent and reaffirm my philosophy of living my intuitive dreams, even while awake.

Most people buy into the idea that growing up requires them to leave their inner child in the dust and assume responsibility as an "adult." However, true growth means listening to your intuition, which in turn requires you to listen to your inner child. And this wild child loves to play—to reenergize with no attached agenda. Why would it make sense to leave the childlike qualities of play, wonder, and joy behind? Humans are meant to play throughout their lives: to explode in laughter, blissfully smile as bare feet touch the grass, marvel at flowers, climb trees, or get lost in playing with a friend. Many of us have trouble unplugging from our techy toys, instead allowing them to eat into our thoughts, self-expression, connection with others, and playtime.

Making play a priority is ironically a very serious issue because many Americans suffer from depression and anxiety. Why does our anxious culture feel the urgency to respond to a text message while at coffee with a friend, or binge on TV shows after work instead of checking in with ourselves? We say we don't have time and convince ourselves the right way is always quick, easy, and efficient. Well, playtime is affordable, quick preventive medicine *and* fuels intuition. It's what keeps us going when we encounter tragedy or trials. So after three years of being sick, I played like I never had before. Play became my medicine. One of my favorite prescriptions is taking a stroll outside while listening to music and appreciating the beauty of flowers. Your form of therapeutic play is probably pretty simple too. Play is really self-love, nourishing juice to keep you living your unique spark. Consistently playing and keeping your inner child alive isn't something to be left behind at adulthood, but rather a lifelong practice of Divine responsibility.

Just like the wilderness found in nature, we all have our own "inner wilderness" to explore and an adult responsibility to clear out the restrictive weeds we've collected throughout our lives thus far. Growing up means having the courage to face our limiting destructive patterns toward ourselves, others, and our relationship with the world and replace them with new patterns that set our inner love-bug up for joy. Through my exploration I realized that the moments in which I feel the most peaceful and free are when I am giving love and receiving love—free from my swirling mind loops and societal expectations of "succeeding" in order to achieve "happiness." You can't "do" happy. You can only "be" happy. I wake up every morning extremely successful just from breathing me. To tend to this inner peace, I practice radical self-compassion and unconditional acceptance, gratefulness for the magic surrounding me, and balance between Divine patience and bold-hearted action. I use my inner child's fearful thoughts as signposts that point me toward love and light once I've lovingly cared for the cute monster under the bed.

To connect with your intuition, you must create a space that your inner child fancies and invite her out for some play. Choose an environment that allows you to feel present, connected to yourself and your surroundings at the same time. Some describe this as a feeling of oneness or outrageous openness. My inner child loves nature. I like to take leisurely nature strolls and flower gaze, hike, bike, lay in the sun, or feel the vibration of a friend's goofy laugh or live music pulsing through my body—anything that engages my senses usually shifts me into Present gear.

The right form of meditation can also create space for intuition. Doing the traditional seated meditation did not work for me because it took me out of my body, so I created my own active joy meditations-in-motion. For me, I enter a euphoric, free-of-thoughts consciousness from doing a creative release activity. My more obvious meditative creative release is my art, which reminded me that meditation can stem from a childhood activity. Creative release is like a massage that softens us up to receive intuition. Creative release occurs outside Ego Land and effortlessly clears out low vibes like fear, sadness, or anger to make room for Divine inspiration. Active joy meditation has many forms. It could be anything you do without thinking that connects you to your sweet, timeless bliss state—for example, ritually drinking tea or coffee solo or with a friend, dancing, playing or listening to music, enjoying a performance, painting or cooking, or even going on an adventure. The important thing to consider in reconnecting with your intuition is to find what naturally makes you feel present. Then, your inner child will come out and play.

We are all given this insanely accurate ability to co-create with the magic of the Universe from our intuitive compass. If you're finding yourself in conflict, it probably means you're not giving enough unconditional love to your Body, Mind, or Spirit; in other words, you are probably not following your inner child's guidance or releasing childhood patterns that are still limiting you. Usually we have what we believe we deserve or what we think we can handle.

Our thoughts create our reality. It is our responsibility to figure out what aspects we're not on board with and then *proactively do* something about them. You don't have to have a physical illness to be unwell or some intense life interrupter to listen to your inner-child; everyone goes through cycles of imbalance and harmony in mind, body, and spirit.

The trick lies in constantly checking in with your intuition. We all experience moments or situations when logic is absent. Instead of feeling powerless, connect into your intuition and you will receive the exact guidance you need to your answer. If you keep your inner child happy, your intuition will pour forth. If you treat 'er with Love and Light, she will carry you along your most authentic loving adventure. Carve out solo intuition time and you'll start hearing the loving whispers toward Mind-Body-Spirit harmony. These loving whispers will get you through the woods. Cheers to your adventure, friend.

ABOUT THE AUTHOR: Born in Dallas, Texas, Christina grew up spending time around the world. She received her B.A. in Sociology from the University of Southern California, and became very involved in holistic creative programs for at-risk youth and juvenile offenders. After being certified in Integrative Nutrition, she channeled her passion for color and soul therapy into her business, HeartArt, which she is currently expanding through writing, Aura Soma, and color-puncture. She believes in intuition as a guiding Life force, the potent remedy of unconditional love, play as medicine, and nature as a best friend.

Christina Dietz
HeartArt
ChristinaDietzArt.com
ChristinaDietzArt@gmail.com
214-763-7013

Find the Feel Good
Sue Urda

Everything is energy and that's all there is to it. Match the frequency of the reality you want and you cannot help but get that reality. It can be no other way. This is not philosophy. This is physics. ~Albert Einstein

The Senses

"The tag on this shirt is driving me crazy." "I have to get these pants off; the seams are really bugging me." These are phrases I've said more often than I care to think about over the past 20 years or so. It seems that my skin has become super-sensitive to the feel and texture of whatever it comes in contact with. I can't even count how many tops I've thrown away after trying to cut out or rip out a tag that was simply too "rough" for me to wear. The feeling is almost like a bug crawling on me or that it's simply rubbing me the wrong way. Other times, the unbearable times, it feels like the tag is actually cutting me—and although I know intellectually this is probably not the case, the feeling is undeniable.

The good news is that I also feel the silkiness, softness, and exquisiteness of fabrics to a high degree, so at least there are some benefits.

"Do you smell that?" This is another question I ask often. I've always had a good sense of smell and in the past years my olfactory system has really heightened. As you can imagine sometimes this is a good thing and others, not so much!

"It's really bright out today, isn't it?" I say as I shade my already sunglass-wearing eyes. Yep, this is another phrase I utter all too often. I find myself squinting when I'm outside to block out the sunlight, and I have a deep crease between my brows that has gotten even deeper since moving to Florida four years ago. Thank goodness for sunglasses and shade.

The Body

In addition to the senses, I have a great need to be comfortable. Now you might say that everyone wants to be comfortable and I know that's true—at least to a degree. Yet, I see women who stand in three-inch heels for a whole day in the name of fashion, and they end up with blisters, bunions, or worse. I have watched people sit on hard chairs through a three-hour meal, and then have to rub their behinds or shake the pins and needles from their legs when they stand up. I've witnessed people sweating in the hot sun refusing to sit under an umbrella or go inside where there's air-conditioning— even though these options are available.

I'm not saying I haven't done all these things myself at one time or another; I just haven't done them lately, because they feel like torture to me. I've had people roll their eyes at me or tell me I don't feel what I feel. How would they know?

Although this high sensitivity isn't always comfortable and I've had to make some changes in my life to accommodate it, in a roundabout way I believe I asked for it.

The Quest for Feeling Good

As I've delved more deeply into personal development and spiritual growth over the past twenty years, I've had this increasing desire to feel good, no matter what. Spiritual teachers like Abraham-Hicks, Marianne Williamson, Louise Hay, Anthony Robbins, Wayne Dyer, and so many others have taught me to be more aware of everything around me and within me, and to choose those things that serve me and make me happy, so that in turn I will be better able to be of service to others. Personal development teachers have taught me that I must focus my thoughts, set my intentions, and develop a mindset that is open and looks for opportunities so I am ready when they show up.

I have discovered the beautiful Spirit that resides within me, and I have learned to nurture it, tap into it, and share it with others. This includes being highly aware of how I'm feeling at any given time and adjusting to be sure the feelings I have are ones I enjoy. One of my forever quests is to raise my mood, attitude, and vibration, because when I'm in this space I am more receptive to the good that is available to me.

In the early 90s when I was working with my dad in our business, he used to say, "If it doesn't feel good, don't do it." Among other things, he was referring to working with certain clients and choosing what part of the business we wanted to work in. Dad was all about "enjoying the process" and I found it so refreshing to work with him after having worked at corporate jobs and with some managers I didn't necessarily enjoy. I can directly attribute at least part of my quest to "find the feel good" to my dad, and even though he left the planet 22 years ago, I still hear his voice in my head, feel him in my heart, and miss him so very much. To this day, when I think of my dad, the most vivid memories are of him making us all laugh, telling me how "outstanding" I was—he even gave me a pin with the word on it, and of his never-ending smile.

Over the years I've developed my own sense of what it means to enjoy the process, and much of it has to do with my surroundings—including the people I have in my life, the physical space that I work, live, and spend time in, and the energy that surrounds me.

I'm Surrounded

Expansive is the way I want to feel. I want to be able to expand my heart, mind, and senses. In order to do this, I choose surroundings that help me feel this way. For example, I love wide open spaces. The greatest place for me to feel expansive is at the beach. When I stand on the sandy shores with the gentle waves lapping at my feet, looking out onto the vast ocean I am nourished, healed, and open. I feel whole. Standing there or sitting in a beach chair I feel completely at one with Mother Nature, Universe, God. I feel connected and free at the same time, and I know that my vibration is raised because I feel light, happy, and deeply grateful.

Since I can't logically spend all my time at the beach, I've found ways to mimic those feelings in the choice of my home, places I visit, and even in choosing where I sit in a room.

There are times I've walked into a restaurant, looked around, noticed the service staff, and walked right back out, because it simply didn't feel "right" to me. The tables may have been oddly arranged or unorganized, the lighting was either too dim or too bright, the staff was loud, rude, or inattentive—any of these things would disturb the vibe and intuitively I knew it would not be an optimal experience for me. Of course, there were times I couldn't leave because of the people I was with, and I always made the best of it, and yet I am usually right on with my gut instincts and have a less than favorable experience. I've also asked to change my table to one that suits my mood, isn't too noisy, has good lighting, and one that looks and "feels" comfy to me, because I know this enhances our overall experience.

Having moved six times in as many years, I've had the opportunity to experience many different types of homes and various surroundings. Renting furnished homes for much of this time, after clearing out my own clutter, was a decision that Kathy and I made so we could find an ideal new home to purchase. The rentals varied greatly, and yet they all had a common thread—from a huge, older house directly on the Jersey shore during the winter off-season, to a modern and stylish three-story on the Cape May bay, to a condo across from the Gulf of Mexico in Marco Island, to living in a newly built guest house overlooking a private pond in Florida, and to staying in a luxury condo on a golf course with a view of the man-made lake. Perhaps it is the water sign in me that always looked for and found a home close to water; what I know is that no matter the home, the water made it feel expansive to me. They all felt like freedom.

When I'm in a space that feels good to me I feel more creative, peaceful, and even healthier. I find it important to follow the basic principles of feng shui, keeping the clutter to a minimum, allowing for the free flowing of walkways, air, and chi, and to decorate in colors, fabrics, lighting, and comfortable practical furniture that support my personal energy. I do the same with the people in my life.

Connections are the Essence of Life

This is a tagline that we use often in our company and network, and I used to call myself the Connections Expert, because it is a focus of my work. I find it really easy to read people and to intuitively know if they are a good fit as a business partner, friend, and alliance or if it's better for me to not get too close. There have been times I ignored my heart instinct because my head was saying logically that someone was a good fit for our business, and sure enough it backfired and we ended our relationship in a not so pleasant way. Sometimes these relationships even caused me to suffer physical discomfort and 'dis-ease' too. Oh, if only I had listened to myself…

I choose to surround myself with people who nurture and support me, ones that I enjoy, and overall those who have a positive, collaborative outlook on life. I find that people who are negative complainers often gravitate to others who are like themselves—and yet sometimes they gravitate towards people like me who look on the bright side. I think this happens because they want what we have—to feel good, and positive, and light—even though they might not fully understand why. I know why though…because positivity feels good, and at a base level "good" is how we all want to feel.

Everything is Energy

Honoring my natural tendencies and honing in on what feels good and what doesn't is an ongoing journey that is becoming increasingly easier. Things change, energy shifts, and even my own needs are ever-evolving. The same people and things that felt good in my 20s and 30s don't necessarily work for me now. I am highly attuned to my own senses and heart space as well as my needs and desires. I recognize more quickly when things are good for me and I swiftly move towards them.

It seems almost cliché to say "I really like her energy," and yet recognizing this has been a cornerstone of my business partnerships and friendships.

Along my journey of growth and development my ability to be in tune with the energy of people, spaces, and everything that surrounds me has served me well. My heightened senses have opened a new level of understanding and awareness for me, and I actively engage my physical, emotional, and ethereal senses to guide me to what is in my highest and best good. This awareness has led me to pursue my purpose and mission of helping people "find the feel good and live in that space every day". The really cool thing is that in fulfilling this purpose to help others, it brings me more into alignment with my own feel good place—and it's really beautiful here.

ABOUT THE AUTHOR: Sue Urda is the Feel Good Guidess. She is an Award-Winning and #1 Bestselling Author, Speaker, Inspirer, and Co-Founder of Powerful You! Women's Network & Powerful You! Publishing. Sue is a two-time honoree on INC Magazine list of the 500 Fastest-Growing Private Companies. Having started three companies since 1989, Sue knows the challenges and joys businesses face, and she is committed to helping entrepreneurs and all women thrive, get connected, share their stories, and feel good. Sue loves assisting individuals in their own pursuit of success, purposeful-living and freedom, and her mission is to connect women to each other, their visions and themselves.

Sue Urda
Feel Good Guidess
Powerful You! Women's Network
Powerful You! Publishing
PowerfulYou.com

Bear Medicine:
Neighbors Helping Neighbors
Kathy Sipple

"Trees are sanctuaries. Whoever knows how to speak to them, whoever knows how to listen to them, can learn the truth. They do not preach learning and precepts, they preach, undeterred by particulars, the ancient law of life." ~ Hermann Hesse

It's December 30th, the no man's land between Christmas and New Year's, especially for those of us who are working. I sit at my desk in my home office and try to be productive, all the while thinking about New Year's Eve plans. I am startled from my reverie as I read the new email on my computer screen:

"I just wanted to thank you for your interest in speaking at TEDx. We interviewed a very competitive pool of applicants, and unfortunately you were not selected to speak at this year's event..."

What?!? How could this be? The last I'd heard from the organizers, they thought my initial presentation was great. They simply suggested that I narrow the focus a bit before returning for a second interview. I knew the brevity of a TED talk would be a challenge for me, and if the invitation for a second interview had not been extended, I would have understood. But the fact that they had extended that invitation, only to rip the rug out from under me later, is very upsetting. As I stare at the email, I move quickly from disappointment to anger. I love listening to TED talks and had already imagined myself onstage, inspiring others with my topic, social permaculture. I wanted to show how ideas of permaculture (a portmanteau of permanent and agriculture, but also culture), can also be applied to human social systems, to much benefit. Admittedly, though my topic was chosen with an idea of helping the planet, there was definitely a healthy dose of ego that wanted the credential of "TED speaker."

I decide a snowy hike in the woods of a nearby park might do me good. Connecting with nature has always been a tonic for my soul. When I earned my Indiana Master Naturalist certification last year, it enriched my existing knowledge, but instead of making me feel like a master, it instilled in me an urgency to learn more and more. I yearned to know about the names and habits of the plants and animals I encountered on these walks. I began paying attention in a deeper way.

Now, as I round the bend near the wetlands, two miles into my route on my chosen hiking path, I smile when I see my special oak tree. I think it looks like a bear, and some years ago took to calling it my "bear tree." It has become my habit to hug my tree every time I pass it.

The tree often communicates with me during these hugs. Rather than spoken words, I "feel" the tree's messages delivered directly to my heart and I know they are not my own thoughts. Once, a few years ago, the tree offered, "Come, Unity. Community." I had never thought of breaking down the word community in that way—either it was the tree's thought form or else the tree inspires a very particular type of creativity in me, maybe both... Typically there are just a few words to the message, but today is different! I feel a pulsing during the hug, as if the tree has a heartbeat and it is in sync with my own. During this "pulsing" I also sense a oneness and a question from the tree: "Will you partner with me to bring bear medicine from the forest out into the world?" I immediately agree, though I realize as I continue my hike that I have no idea what I had just agreed to. What is bear medicine? I don't know.

Who do I know that would have insights into bear medicine messages from talking trees? I remember a Facebook group I'd joined called The Talking Tree Sisterhood. Within minutes of my reaching out to them, group members offer affirmation and support. One woman comments that "the bear often serves the village in some way;" she also recommends reading, Medicine Cards: The Discovery of Power through the Ways of Animals. When I research the book, one particular passage leaps out at me: "In choosing Bear, the power of knowing has invited you to enter the silence and become acquainted with the Dream Lodge, so that your goals may become concrete realities."

Hmm, what does it all mean? I stand up to stretch and take a break, which includes a walk down to the mailbox and see what's waiting for me there. I step out onto the driveway and immediately slip and fall on just-formed slick black ice. My head and back are already hurting from the contact with the hard, cold cement, but not as badly as my ego, wounded yet again in a single morning. I hope no neighbors heard me yell out in surprise as I fell. Large snowflakes float down and land on my face. I painfully turn on my side, then awkwardly lift myself to my feet.

I have too much to do to be in this much pain, I tell myself,— how will the driveway get shoveled if I'm laid up like this? We are somewhat new in this neighborhood and I don't have anyone to call. "Screw the mail and shoveling," I say finally, "I'm going to hibernate!" This was my first lesson in bear medicine: self-care.

I pop a few aspirins and cuddle up in bed with the vision board I'd created several years ago. Sometimes staring at it reminds me of my bigger purpose and helps me feel better about temporary setbacks. I am astounded to see a picture of a bear in the upper left corner. I don't remember including that. I drift to sleep in minutes and upon waking a few hours later recall my dream...about a bear. Maybe my bear tree and my subconscious are conspiring… I pick up my journal and begin to write. My particular form of bear medicine was suddenly clear—I know I will serve my village by starting a time bank to empower people to heal themselves, each other and our local economy.

Time banking has been around for thirty-plus years, though it is not well known in many places and certainly not in Northwest Indiana where I live. Back in the 80s, I had majored in Economics at the University of Michigan, but while most of my fellow students were setting their sights on Wall Street, I was taking classes on Economics of the Environment, covering topics such as Sustainable Forestry and the Economics of Superfund site cleanup. I also took a rather sobering class called The Economics of Population and learned about several alarming trends, including the challenges our society would face when the population bubble of Baby Boomers hit retirement age in record numbers, beginning in the early 21st century.

Now that time has arrived, and although I'm a GenXer and nowhere near retirement age, I can, especially in my current state of back pain, empathize with an older person who might experience pain or disability as a regular thing. What would they do? Would it be bad enough to force them into a nursing home? What if there were people they could depend on to help fill in the gaps with chores they needed done? Time banking could help, I realize.

The elderly are not the only segment of society that need help—I see how the current system doesn't fully address the needs of non-English-speaking people, people with disabilities, the unemployed, underemployed, and many more. Economic pressures and social isolation are all too common in most communities, and each makes the other worse. What if we get innovative and tap into underutilized resources (that is, skills) which are personal rather than economic? What if we then connect all these resources so everyone is aware of everyone else's skills? Time banking offers a way to recreate social capital (a contemporary need)—much easier than creating financial capital but equally important in order to thrive.

The following weeks flow with a grace previously unknown to me. A local Innovator meetup group finds out about my project and asks me to be the featured speaker the following month. I launch and successfully complete a crowdfunding campaign to cover startup costs and to ensure there is enough interest in the community to support the project. I speak at other community and environmental group functions. I am asked to speak at our local Earth Day celebration and the organizers send out press releases. I am asked to do radio interviews. Notification comes that a local entrepreneurship event called The Big Sell has selected my project to compete in the social entrepreneurship category. A leadership team comes together with ease and grace, nearly all the contacts I reached out to said yes!

"We are the ones we've been waiting for." ~ attributed to an unnamed Hopi elder

Members join and begin to exchange hours with one another. One of my neighbors fixes my mom's computer. The neighbor needs a beekeeping mentor; another member is ready to help out. A young woman with a corporate job dreams of leaving it behind and taking up farming; another fifty-something member offers mentoring and friendship as they tend to her llamas together on her own small farm.

The type of skills shared continues to grow as members discover how the system works and realize how much they have to offer one another. Healthy meals are delivered. Massages are given. A woman whose husband is dying at home under hospice care receives visits and help with grocery delivery.

All these yeses, following the big "no" that had stung so much on that snowy day in December. I realize that if I'd won a coveted spot on the TED stage, I would have spent the past three months perfecting an eighteen-minute speech instead of actually building something that would serve my community in a meaningful way.

Last week I attended the local TEDx event to show my support. I applauded the speakers and found that I did not envy them. I was grateful to be in the audience instead of on the stage...this year. Next year? Look out! The tree and I have some big plans that will have unfolded by then and I'm betting will make for one heck of a compelling TED talk.

ABOUT THE AUTHOR: Kathy Sipple has been studying to become a social alchemist her whole life, though has just recently realized it. She is enrolled in a permaculture design certification program and is documenting the success of CoThrive timebank to illustrate how she has applied social permaculture principles in its creation. When she's not working on the timebank, Sipple works as a social media consultant and trainer and also hosts an award-winning podcast about environmental topics. She lives in Valparaiso, Indiana with her husband John and their black Lab Bodhi. They enjoy frequent hikes at the Indiana Dunes State Park where her beloved bear tree resides.

Kathy Sipple
kathy@cothrive.org
cothrive.org
mysocialmediacoach.com
219greenconnect.com

Creating Home Runs
Glenn Schock

In the summer of 1956, Granny Hamner got caught stealing third base in an important game against the Pittsburgh Pirates. The Philadelphia Phillies had men on first and second base with two away in the eighth inning and were down by one run. Robin Roberts was pitching a two-hitter and the only run was scored on a throwing error. Mayo Smith, the Phillies' manager was kicking the bat rack and throwing equipment all around the dugout. My Grandpop and Uncle Clyde were screaming at the television, because "You never, ever, make the first or last out at third base." That unwritten rule stuck with me, my entire life and was my first recollection of baseball, as a child. From that moment on, I was hooked on Baseball and did everything I could to learn as much about the sport as possible. I wanted to join in on those heated conversations that took place every Sunday afternoon at Pop Pop's when the Phillies were playing.

I read the Reading Eagle sports page after every Phillies game and learned about the players, not only the Phillies players, but all the players in the National League. Sundays at Pop Pop's were much more fun now that I knew some baseball facts, but I wasn't coming up with anything that got their attention. I needed a better source of information.

My neighbor, Tommy, was an avid baseball card collector and it was he, who got me interested in card collecting. On the back of each card was the player's statistics from the previous year, career totals plus an interesting anecdote about the players, teams or rules. What a great way to get into the Sunday game chatter. A pack of cards with a slab of bubble gum sold for a nickel at Eshellman's Grocery store. My main source of income was returning soda bottles for our neighbor, Aida Meyer, as long as I gave her half the money. If I was going to accumulate enough cards to supply me with baseball facts, I needed to find a better way to make some cash, fast.

When school let out in June of 1957, my plan was to set up a Kool-Aid stand and sell cups of Kool-Aid to the Moms as they walked by on their way to the grocery store. Unfortunately, Linda Devine, who lived across the street and was three years older, had a stand set up, while I was still in the planning stages. She was cleaning up and I was broke. I decided to play on the dirt pile, next to the construction site, where new homes were being built. Three homes were being built on the next street and the dirt pile was the result of the foundations being excavated. I was sliding down the pile on a cardboard box when I heard an argument between some of the carpenters and their boss. The carpenters were upset because the coffee guy hadn't come at lunchtime and the carpenters were yelling at the foreman to get them drinks.

I saw this as my big opportunity to make some fast money. I went home and filled two Coleman picnic jugs with cold well water and I cracked a tray of ice cubes in each jug. I put them in my Radio Flyer wagon along with some Dixie cups and pulled my wagon up to the building site. The foreman was standing next to his truck, puffing on a cigar and writing on a clipboard. He had a big bushy mustache and a red plaid shirt rolled up to the elbows, which showed the tattoos on his arms. The closer I got to him, the bigger he looked. When I got next to him, I was afraid to say anything.

"What do you want, kid?" he said, as he tossed his clipboard on the front seat of his truck. "I brought water for the men", I said with my hands in my pockets. "Do you have cups", he barked as he puffed on his cigar. I held up a stack of cups. The foreman pulled a brass whistle out of his pocket and blew it three times. All hammering stopped. He yelled, "The kid has water, give him a quarter, he'll give you a cup." He then said to me, "Stand over there and only give them a cup if they give you a quarter, got it?" I nodded and began passing out cups. It wasn't long before all my cups were gone and I was holding my shorts up so they wouldn't fall down. My pockets were pretty full of coins. A lot of the guys gave me pennies. When the water was empty, I looked at the foreman and shrugged my shoulders.

The foreman told me to call him Mike and said, "Pick up the cups and come back tomorrow at ten o'clock and again at three in the afternoon, okay?" It took me about ten minutes to pick up the used cups, as I had to hold up my shorts with one hand.

On the way home, I stopped at the grocery and had to listen to Mister Eshellman tease me about my shorts falling down. I bought two boxes of Dixie cups and half a carton of baseball cards. Mr. Eshellman asked me if my Mother knew I was spending all this money. I yelled, "she knows all about it" as I pushed open the screen door and left the store. I opened 4 packs of cards in front of the store and began chewing the slabs of bubble gum as I flipped through the new cards. After reading several cards, I walked home, pulling my wagon and waved hello to Linda. I smiled, knowing I made more money than she and tomorrow would even be better.

The next morning, I got to the building site at 10 o'clock, Mike said some of the men only got one cup full before my water ran out. I told him I only had two water jugs. He said give them a cup for a dime and see how it goes. I was disappointed about the price reduction. After all, Mike had set the price at a quarter. Mike blew his brass whistle an announced the new price of ten cents. Most of the guys gave me a quarter, anyway, which was fine with me. Mike gave me a dollar bill and when I tried to give him change, he told me to keep it. He reminded me to clean up the paper cups and come back at 3 o'clock. I sold ice water to the carpenters, every day, from Monday through Friday until the first week in August, when our family went to Wildwood at the Jersey Shore for two weeks vacation. I really wanted to stay home and make money with my new enterprise.

I don't remember how much money my little project earned, but I was able to collect the entire set of 1957 baseball cards, which gave me lots of topics for discussion with Uncle Clyde and Pop Pop as well as plenty of cash to play skeeball on the boardwalk. When we came home from vacation the three homes were finished, the dirt pile was gone and Mike and the carpenters would not be coming back.

I was proud of my accomplishments for my first entrepreneurial venture and didn't seriously get into anything steady until I was ten years old, when I started mowing lawns and doing yard work and other odd jobs, like shoveling snow. I built a weather station, from a Heath kit, which would activate my alarm clock, when it snowed. I had four driveways, including ours to clean on weekdays before 7 o'clock. I always had something going to earn money. My newspaper route paid for my weekly trip to the movies. I never turned down a babysitting job because that was free money for watching television and doing my homework. As a teenager I painted fences and washed and waxed cars. I even built a spray booth in our garage and painted a few cars. There was always money to be made, if you took the time to look for an opportunity.

My first real job was without a doubt, my favorite job of all. I was hired as a part-time copyboy for a local newspaper. My job was to pick up bags of mail at the post office, sort and pass out the correspondence, run errands for the editors, meet reporters to pick up stories, pick up the Police Blotters at three different municipal stations, pass out galley sheets for proofreading, and most importantly pick up coffee and sandwiches for the editorial staff, reporters, and printers. As long as I got everything done, I was able to study, do homework, anything I wanted. Within six months I was filling in for the obituary lady when she called out, writing articles for the Sunday Edition Science section, cartooning, and working in the photo lab and engraving lab. I was the go-to guy when something needed to get done.

It's amazing how opportunities present themselves, if you pay attention. A long time friend called me one afternoon and asked me for my opinion on a business venture. The business was buying products that you use every day from your own store and selling the idea to others. Every time a product was purchased, you would get a set percentage. Customers would earn you a small income, but if you could sell the idea to others, you would get paid on every sale they made as well. The concept was interesting and I took the plunge. My outgoing personality made it easy for me to introduce this concept to others and in a few months, I was earning a nice second income. The problem was the people that I recruited to sell the idea to others were unable to consistently recruit like me and quit soon thereafter due to slow sales.

Network Marketing only works when everything is correctly in place. The products have to be excellent, the pay plan has to be fair for everyone (the part timers need to make a decent income as well as the heavy hitters), there has to be a good market for the products, and the owners of the company have to be ethical. Take one item away and the concept loses steam and failure is a foregone conclusion.

After working four different opportunities with my wife Dale—who I affectionately call Sweetie—we found a company that seemed to have it all. We were rolling along, earning good checks, developing a strong organization, and training our people to duplicate the process. For some crazy reason, the owners of the company decided they needed to keep a larger piece of the pie. We were notified that the pay plan was being enhanced and within a month my very nice commission check dropped by eighty percent. I knew it wouldn't be long before everything fell apart. While the meltdown was in the works, Sweetie and I had been learning about toxin-free products from one of the product developers. We had been organizing trainings on the east coast to teach our Associates about those products, their ingredients, the science involved, and how to use them effectively.

When we left that opportunity, we decided to develop our own line of toxin-free products and salvage some of our faithful organization. We developed a line of nine products and launched a new company. The products were amazing and to get the business into high gear we took on a partner to help with the funding. Eventually, we sold our involvement in that venture due to a difference of opinion in the way we wanted to operate.

We decided to start over, take our time and run the business the way we would be most comfortable. We restarted as AlphaZelle in 2004 with just a few personal care products. It was important to us that our ingredients were USDA Certified Organic or Wild Crafted, and we teach our customers how to read labels so they can eventually become toxin-free. Our website, AlphaZelle.com features a learning center to help guide our customers towards a toxin-free lifestyle.

It wasn't long before we began expanding our lines. We now have over eighty products, including Pure Basics (fifty-nine personal care products), Pure Baby (eight products for Mommies and Babies), Pure Pet (eight Pet products), and Pure Home (five cleaning and laundry products). AlphaZelle will soon be introducing a line of therapeutic, food grade essential oil blends, presently in the test marketing stages, because my research has shown that essential oils, when blended effectively can eliminate many toxic drugs and address the causes, rather than the symptoms of so many issues.

I've always loved being my own boss and identifying opportunities came easy for me. I must admit they all haven't been winners, but they definitely were learning experiences. Sweetie and I have been following our hearts for many years and have taken the plunge whenever an opportunity felt right. Our decision to start and grow AlphaZelle has been a blessing and the right thing to do and truly feels like a home run.

ABOUT THE AUTHOR: Having been his own boss from the age of seven Glenn relies heavily on his own educational ventures over traditional studies. He excelled early in his career, creating organization and training for techs in a plastic stabilizer manufacturing company that led to company accolades. In the spirit of entrepreneurship, Glenn partnered to start a delivery company that blossomed into a thriving meat sales company until 1995 when he left to pursue direct sales. Being community minded, Glenn was a volunteer fireman for ten years, and served as a board member of his community for thirty years with five years as President. Glenn now serves AlphaZelle as a researcher, copywriter consultant, and is studying to be a Certified Aromatherapist.

Glenn R Schock
Advocate for Toxin-Free Living
AlphaZelle LLC
alphazelle.com
glenn@alphazelle.com

A Compass 2 Life

One Woman's Journey from Living Empty to Dying Empty
Suzanne Spencer

I am always in awe when my husband talks about his earliest childhood memories, all the way back to the age of four. Yet at the same time I am haunted by my inability to conjure up any of my own memories as a young child. There was no overt abuse or trauma in my life, but for some reason those memories are absent from my reservoir. Throughout the years, I have examined reoccurring dreams, fears, and behavioral patterns, yet the question remains unanswered. With few exceptions, the years before the age of eleven are simply a blank.

Oddly enough, the trauma came two years later, when the long-ignored problems in my parents' marriage finally came to a head. After the divorce, my father got custody of me and my two younger brothers—a blessing, given my mother's signs of alcoholism and depression. Her threats of impending doom and punishment for my existence had instilled in me a host of fears. After all, if a mother could not love you, then who else in the world possibly could? I clung to my father, afraid that he would see my mother in me and "divorce" me too.

As my parents had often fought about me, I also felt guilty that I caused their breakup; in fact, I felt responsible for the decisions and behaviors of everyone in my life. My inner world became full of turmoil and "rules" by which I had to live, so much so that I wondered whether I was going crazy. I read "Sybil," the seminal work on multiple personalities, and thought it sounded like me, for I often felt like two completely different people. One was the outer face I showed to the world, happy and confident; the other believed it was wrong to have needs or that one should rise above them (and certainly never voice them); this personality wanted to be invisible. Underneath both was a vast, dark emptiness, a bottomless pit that nothing could fill.

The Dichotomy

Now, back to that first personality, that vibrant outer self I skillfully projected to the world. I had the most glamorous, flowing beauty queen hair (Revlon got all my paychecks). Later, at the age of twenty-one, I stood on the stage at the Miss World Pageant to represent the British Virgin Islands as one of the eighty-four most beautiful women that year and was a role model for young girls all over the world. Ironically, while I was busy telling them how they should be like me, I did not even want to be me. I was a size zero (that magic number admired by so many women); I was glamorous with my walk, I was exotic in my look. I was both a threat and an inspiration to women and viewed as an object of desire for men. Yet inside I was a mass of contradictions: the center of attention yet alone in a room full of people, I distracted others by my exterior yet yearned for a deeper connection; I attracted all eyes on me, yet I dreaded people looking at me. I longed for a relationship, yet feared intimacy; I had an ego but no self- esteem. I had no sense of self but was defined by others' perceptions.

Living Empty

The same year, those contradictions collided when at the age of twenty-one I was diagnosed with anorexia. While I had been suffering with the disorder since thirteen, the stress of the Miss World Pageant had turned out to be the final straw. The ensuing breakdown forced me to return to my father and stepmother's house in Canada. I was completely starved, not only in my body, but in my mind, heart, and soul. The black hole of emptiness was threatening to consume me, and worst of all, no one understood my despair. There were many moments I wanted to die, yet there was always a small flame deep within me that fought to live and to carry on. Now, thirty-five years later, I look back on my life and realize that even when my faith was at my weakest I could feel that little ember inside, fighting to hold on. Somehow, I intuitively knew that if I could make it to the age of twenty-five I would have a chance at a long life. For some reason twenty-five was the magic number upon which the rest of my life would be determined. As I write this I am forty-eight, and made it beyond the magic of a number not only in my age but on the scale, in my self- worth, and in God given value.

Saving My Life

It's hard when you are in the throes of something to see the small steps of progress and growth. I spent twenty years in the grip of anorexia, every minute of which was taking me closer to my grave. In the early 80s there was very little known about the disease except for Karen Carpenter's highly publicized struggle with it. There we no treatment centers like today, just hospital psych wards full of people with severe mental health issues. Eating disorder patients received "cognitive behavior therapy," meaning you were held in a closet-sized room with a nurse and four other girls who were highly dosed on Ativan to help ward off anxiety. Only after thousands of calories had been consumed could patients return to the common area. Bathrooms remained locked to prevent vomiting. While others on the ward were running from demons in their mind, rocked themselves to disassociation and screamed in the middle of the night, I was simply a girl who was trying not to take up space in the world, to find a way to get rid of the "needs" inside me so that I could be a better daughter, a better sister, a better student, a better anything that anyone needed me to be. Again, that internal flame came to my rescue, reminding me this was not the path to healing.

Just shy of two months and against the advice of my doctors and family members, I checked myself out of the hospital. I was determined to find another way to heal, a way in which I took a more active role. I started going to the Toronto library, reading and learning about this thing trying to consume me. I combed the phonebook for therapists and finally found a child psychologist from Australia willing to take my case. He would spend years helping me and my family to save our lives. With his guidance, I started becoming aware of the unhealthy decisions I was making and the reasons for them. This was the first step in recognizing that I had choices and understanding that there could be boundaries between myself and others. Once I realized that boundaries are less about saying no to others and more about saying yes to myself, I began to feel comfortable establishing and maintaining these boundaries, which in turned empowered me to fill my own space and respect my core values.

One of the most critical aspects of the healing process was learning to use my voice. Given my history of trying to starve myself, it was the most difficult. First, I had to recognize that I even *had* a voice. I did this by acknowledging and validating my emotions; for example, anger was a sign that I had an unmet need. Again, this was a tough one for me, for while in the throes of my eating disorder I tried to starve and suffocate my needs.

The second step was starting to use that voice. It was certainly awkward at first; my voice had been ignored for so long that it sometimes came out uncontrolled, uncensored and aggressive. I had to learn to not judge myself, but to accept this as an important part of the healing process.

Eventually, I was ready to move on to the third and most important step, which was learning to use my voice *effectively* in order to get my needs met. Achieving this was the result of my finding balance between my needs and the needs of the person I was communicating with.

Also critical to my healing was learning how to transcend fear. For most of my youth, I was overcome with fear, mostly about my abilities. I believed I was incapable and incompetent and was constantly afraid I would be found out. The hardest part was that I thought I was the only one ruled by fears. Later, my father told me that the fear I felt was not unique to me; in fact, what made me different was that I felt the fear and did it anyway.

I also learned to embrace the "Be versus Better" concept. After years of struggling to be "better", I began to wonder, who I was competing with, who was this invisible person I needed to be better than? How come regardless of what I did or how much I achieved, I never arrived at this sense of better? And, anyway, what was the point, when the person right behind me could easily bump me out of the slot? Working toward "better" had been a torment for me; I had to learn to "be" my best self.

Finding my core values was another aspect of healing that involved an enormous amount of work and willingness to change. After years of listening to the controlling and abusive voices in my head, I needed to take back control by finding out what truly mattered to me. Words like integrity and honesty seemed trite; I needed words that I felt passionate about. It took fifteen years, but I eventually found five core values I could hang my hat on. Even today, these values are symbolic of who I am today as a person, who I have in my life, how I conduct myself, the choices I make, and the way I own the space I now know I deserve in the world.

Consciousness

After years of suffering and gut-wrenching struggle, I finally emerged as a confident woman who can either command a crowded room or be by herself in an empty one. I knew my value to the workplace, to my family, to my community, to the world, and to God. I knew what was most important to me and I was willing to stand by those choices in all I did. I went back to school to get my Masters in Leadership; I also became a representative of one of our most vulnerable populations—those struggling with substance abuse and addiction. Once without a voice, I am now recognized for its ability to represent not only myself, but those who are vulnerable and unable to represent themselves.

That didn't mean it was always easy. I lost friends, had to leave jobs, and made tough choices that were in line with my priorities but were not always understood by those around me. Yet for the first time, I was authentic in my look, thought, and deed. I was living fully—emotionally, spiritually, and physically. In the process, I also met and married the man of my dreams and gave birth to our son. At the age of forty-three, I had become the parent I needed and wanted as a young child and adult. My transformation had come full circle.

Dying Empty

It took me years to fill the void inside me, but as I look back now I realize that there is some value to being empty, just not in the way I did it. Like me, too many people are *living* empty—they starve their needs and disconnect from intimacy; they engage in friendships and careers not aligned with their true selves. Humans are designed for connection, yet isolation is a growing epidemic. Everywhere it is said people are anesthetizing themselves— numbing, stuffing, self-medicating.

When I talk about being empty, I am talking about dying empty: knowing that whenever you may be called upon to take your last breath, you can leave knowing that you gave and left this world with every contribution to its betterment that you had to give. That you used your talents and gifts, that you were active in sharing them, that your voice represented your needs and those of others, that you left our children with the tools they need to survive and thrive, and that you were fill with gratitude rather than regret. Strange as it may sound, I believe our world would be a much better place if we "died empty." I certainly hope I do.

ABOUT THE AUTHOR: Suzanne is a speaker, thought leader, and consultant committed to building companies, teams, and people through virtuous leadership. Recognized as a "visionary" in the Recovery industry, she continues to collaborate with non-profits to provide strategic planning, program development, training and recruitment, fundraising, and transformational leadership. A lifelong learner, Suzanne is currently working toward her Masters in Leadership and is always open to "kairos" moments that allow her to remain teachable while helping to grow others.

Suzanne Spencer
Compass2Life Inc.
suzannespencer.biz
Consulting@suzannespencer.biz

Journey of Re-Creation
Carly Alyssa Thorne

Throughout my life, I have been asked why and how I am so positive and live with so much energy and passion. Well, my journey from "SOS" to CAT is a long one, and if you choose to take it with me, you will understand why I am all about transformation of the Mind, Body, Business, and Spirit, and why I live to empower, motivate, inspire, and educate myself and others each and every day.

My intention is that after reading this you will be able to "choose you," maybe for the first time in your life. You will be able to say to yourself, Yes, I can! I can have a healthy mind-body-spirit and business; I can create a team to support me, and I can support others; I can stand in my power and be strong and still be compassionate; I can be in gratitude for each and every day; I can forgive self and others; and I can reach out and get the help and education necessary to thrive.

You will also be able to look in the mirror and say to yourself: You are Loved! You are Appreciated! You are Worthy! You are Beautiful! When you can say this to yourself, you will be able to take this out to the world and say it to others.

This is not to say your journey will be a smooth one. Just remember that it is in your darkest times that you will find out who your true friends are; you also find out how amazingly strong, resilient, and powerful you can be when you have the right tools and the right team, tribe, and/or support system to help guide you along the way.

What we focus on expands, therefore I have always used my story as a teaching beacon and a way to help others get through the maze of darkness and into the light. At the end of every tunnel of darkness and pain, there is light; we just have to be willing to sit with, feel, and look for it.

I was born in Yonkers, New York in 1964 and given a name with the initials SOS, which as it would turn out was very symbolic of my life growing up. I was always seeking help, in trouble, confused, and dismayed with life. I had many health, family, and relationship problems. Today, I wouldn't call them problems, I would call them lessons of self-discovery and growth, all of which come with the choice to learn and, ultimately, grow.

When I was five years old I left the United States and went to live first in Mexico, then Venezuela and Brazil. The upheaval continued after we returned to the U.S. when I was fourteen. We lived in several different areas of New York and New Jersey, where for the first time I was introduced to the public school system after years of private Catholic Schools abroad. By the time I graduated high school I had attended nine different schools.

This led to some pretty strong resentment of my circumstances. The constant travel made it difficult to make friends, as I was always the new kid, the outsider. This, however, was the relatively "easy" part of my growing up years. I was also raped repeatedly and endured frequent verbal, sexual, emotional, and physical abuse, eventually resulting in severe Post Traumatic Stress Syndrome. I also had to contend with multiple health issues, including very poor eye sight, depression, severe endometriosis, and advanced degenerative joint bone disease in all major joints. I underwent countless surgeries (I stopped counting after #17, and there were many more after that), and for a long time lived in perpetual crisis mode.

I went through years of treatment, was on many western medicines, and was even hospitalized, twice for suicide attempts. I struggled with weight issues on both ends of the spectrum, weighing just 95 pounds at my worst bout with anorexia to 200 pounds at my heaviest. I went through this cycle three times.

I do not share these things to gain your pity; nor do I share them to stay mired in the past or dwell on it. In fact, I am extremely grateful for my past, for it has made me into the strong, passionate, compassionate, healthy, giving person I am today.

My experiences as a young adult and into adulthood provided me with lessons that I continue to work on each and every day and choose to do so for the rest of my life, including: reaching out; standing up for oneself; forgiving self and others; being in gratitude for each and every day; creating possibilities; having clearing conversations with people; being open and vulnerable; taking down the armor; realizing the power of the tribe and collaboration; realizing that we are all interconnected; truly and fully listening to another; developing compassionate, passionate communication; living from a place of love-peace-gratitude; developing conscious business collaborations; tapping into the multi-sensory self and world; and being open to all feedback, no matter what that feedback is and not reacting-defending, just being with it and choosing what to do with it.

One of the most important things I learned and share with others is that we all have the power to affect the world. Each of us creates a "ripple effect," and race, gender, finances, and/or education is not a barrier to reaching out in whatever way feels right, and with the knowledge that our actions, no matter how small or big, can make a difference in this world, one step, one person at a time.

Today, I am beyond grateful for my journey, including the extensive travel I so resented in my youth. Living in so many different places has enabled me to ebb and flow, adapt to any given environment or situation, and think on my feet. It has taught me to respect many different cultures and acknowledge all beings as individuals on the same soul level, which in turn informs my coaching, mentoring, and teaching. One must come from a place of authentic experience in order to truly and deeply help someone else. Yes, your experience is unique; however, someone can empathize and understand if they have experienced it to some degree in their own life. I am saying this because, as thankful and grateful as I am for my life, it has been far from easy. I look back now and realize the path I was on was one of strength, understanding, and compassion, for myself and others, and to be able to use my gifts to help others get out of their own maze of darkness as I did.

For me, that cycle of darkness and negativity began to break down in 1998, when my husband committed suicide. I had a major choice to make—Do I choose life? Death? Hate? Guilt? Take on the blame everyone was throwing at me? Become the victim? Become and stay a hardened, unfeeling shell?

This agonizing event would turn out to be both my biggest gift and my biggest lesson. My late husband had presented me with a crossroads I could not ignore. Trust me when I tell you that in the moment the choice was far from easy; I had to stand alone, be strong, and let go of all places, things, old friends, family members, and most of all, the stories. I had to stand up to and face the past, stand up to family members and stand firm for choosing me, while at the same time taking full responsibility for my part in the co-creation of it all.

I had to be willing to expose all of my skeletons, demons, fears, and failures, including errors to self and others. I had to let go of all judgments of self and others as well. In short, I had to be willing to show up. Hiding and playing small was no longer an option for me.

Another aha moment that awakened me to how truly precious life is (and how short it can be) occurred on September 11, 2001. At that time I was working at the World Trade Center as a Wellness-Fitness Consultant and Trainer. As one of their specialized medical trainers, I dealt with the clients that had major medical issues. My first client of the day had cancelled our session, as he was spending the day at his beach house. Normally, I would have gone in at the usual time and worked out myself, however, on that morning I decided to leave an hour later. Thanks to this last minute decision I was at the train station and out of harm's way when the Twin Towers were struck. To this day I have my locker keys and pen with the World Trade Center logo, and they never fail to remind me to be grateful for every single day.

Now, does all of this mean my work is done, that I am saved? Not at all. Like everyone else I will always be learning, failing, and discovering. The only difference between then and now is that I work on myself each and every day; I am aware of my potholes and catch myself when I get too close. Then it is time to make a new decision and recommit to love of life, self, and others.

Then comes the inevitable question: how the hell did you get to this place?

Well, first I had to make some HUGE life-changing decisions.

First and foremost, I had to let go of the negative people, places, and things that kept me bound to old, outdated beliefs about who I was and what I could or could not have, be, and do. Next, I had to choose to be around positive, happy, healthy, abundant-minded people, places, and things.

I also had to make the choice to be constantly learning, playing, and growing—every day. I took many self-development courses that expanded my mind, body, and spirit; I read voraciously, studied both Western and Eastern philosophies around wellness, and did things that pushed me out of my comfort zone. I even ate fire and walked on hot coals!

One of the main things I learned was that both Western and Eastern medicine and philosophies serve a purpose and have a place. More importantly, I learned that we are all powerful beyond measure.

After many years and layers of self-discovery, I realized that while my physical issues were most certainly real, I had created much of them as a way of coping with all the fear, anger, and sadness my inner child felt. And at that time the unwillingness to truly forgive self and others for everything that I experienced ate away at the core of my being and affected my mind-body-business and spirit.

These days, I have good healthy collaborative co-creational friendships; the world and the universe is my family. I surround myself with amazing and inspiring teachers, mentors, leaders, and awesome, passionate, powerful souls who live from abundance. And by abundance, I am not just talking about money. I have had a lot of money and I have had very little. I have also re-created abundance in many forms. My lesson around abundance was keeping it, as I tended to spend all my money on others. I believed myself to be the ultimate giver, yet little did I know that this was my covert way of buying people's love and approval. Aha! I also learned I wasn't truly open to receiving because I didn't think I deserved it. It wasn't until I started to shift that consciousness and be open to receiving that things began to turn around.

I now choose each and every day when I wake up to live my life with as much spunk, vigor, happiness, health, and abundance as I can with self and others. And since I want to leave this world better than I found it, I am a huge believer in Paying It Forward (a hand up through education-empowerment-motivation-skills-collaborations, not a hand out) and The Ripple Effect.

Thanks for taking this journey with me. I hope that it has inspired you in some way to say yes to life, to say yes, I am bigger than any of this. Everything has beauty, even within the darkness, if we can be willing to feel and look for the light.

One of my favorite things to end with is inspiring others to realize that every day is a Re-Birth Day, a chance to release the old, outdated thinking and embrace the new. On this day and every day, I wish you many blessings in creating the you, you want to be, do, and become.

ABOUT THE AUTHOR: Carly Alyssa Thorne is a speaker, author, consultant, producer, and director on Conscious Business Collaborations, specializing in multisensory, multimedia, and the mind-body-business-spirit interconnectedness. Carly also has an extensive background in metaphysics and health, having owned and consulted on several healing centers. Carly went on to study and become a Reiki Master Instructor and Integrated Energy Therapy Master Instructor and studied extensively nutrition, aromatherapy, flower essences, herbs, overall health, fitness, and anything she could get her hands on that tied back to the multisensory human beings she believes we are. Carly has worked with individuals, families, and companies on comprehensive health programs and led numerous retreats. Carly believes we are all multisensory, multidimensional beings that are all interconnected.

Carly Alyssa Thorne
Collaborative Empowerment Implementer & Muse
CarlyAlyssaThorne.com
carlyathorne@gmail.com
818-284-6284

Shift the Grid

Manifest Your Goals, Dreams and Aspirations!

Stacy Davenport

From the early age of seven, I learned that if I rearranged my room and the things in it I would find comfort within myself. At that time, I had no idea how vital that connection would be to the successful journey of my life.

Perhaps keeping an orderly space was important because of the chaos surrounding me. My mother suffered from mental illness and was in and out of psychiatric wards and state hospitals throughout my childhood and well into my twenties. I remember one hospitalization in particular. I was four years old, and the three months she was gone seemed like years. Finally, the day came when my dad said, "Stay here with Grandma; I am going to go pick up your mother."

How excited I was to see my mom again! I waited and waited, and just when it seemed they would never arrive, I heard Dad's car pull up to the house. I ran to the front door and screamed, "Mommy!"

For a moment my mother just stood there and stared at me; then she said, "Who are you?"

My little heart shattered into a million pieces. In that instant, the power and presence of God swept in and spoke: "Dear One, I have you from this moment through eternity." Since then, I have forever trusted my connection with God, who I now refer to as The Divine.

It was not until many years later that I learned why my mom didn't know me. During her time in the mental hospital she had been given shock therapy. This experience was both a curse and a blessing, for as painful as it was, it led me to pursue a greater understanding of life.

From then on, when my outer life became chaotic, rearranging my room was a way of restoring order and resetting my connection with The Divine, once again.

At twenty-one, I began my spiritual journey in order to discover and understand the pain, chaos and abandonment that I was experiencing—for the purpose of healing it. In 1992, I was led to pick up Sarah Rossbach's *Feng Shui – Ancient Chinese Wisdom on Arranging a Harmonious Living Environment*. It was my first book on the topic, and it would prove to be a game-changer.

As I read the book, I soon began to understand that at seven years old I had actually been feng shuiing my bedroom, and that doing so had helped me process painful experiences. It made me wonder what feng shui could help me accomplish as an adult. At this time, I was working in corporate America, so I set the energy and a strong intention in the abundance, money, and power section of my home. My intention was to receive a $200 month raise. Within two weeks, I received a $250 month raise and a $5,000 bonus! "Don't tell anyone about this," my boss told me, "This is only for you." It was intended as a reward for my hard work at the office; however, I knew that this unexpected income was really the result of my working with and activating the energy of my home.

Now that feng shui had gotten my attention, signs kept showing up to let me know I was on the right path. Most importantly, I was led to phenomenal teachers such as Master Lin Yun in Berkeley, California, along with James Moser and Sean Xenja, and I eagerly soaked up as much of their knowledge as I could.

In 1996, I was certified in the ancient principles and systems of feng shui. It was as if I had been given a golden tool box, into which I would be able to put all the tools and processes that I had gained throughout my journey and use them to support others in their lives. Since then, I have continued collecting tools and adding them to my tool box. I was trained in dowsing and recalibrating the energy grid and eventually began combining these two powerful systems to provide powerful and effective shifts within personal, business, and school environments. I also became a Certified Life Coach, Akashic Records Consultant, and Life Purpose Hand Analyst. I refer to this set of tools as my four-legged stool, because no matter what service a client is seeking when he/she comes in to work with me, the other three areas can support their transformation.

At the time of this writing I have energetically cleared, recalibrated, and feng shui'd more than 3,600 spaces. I have also touched thousands of individuals—locally, nationally, and internationally. While much of my work is conducted in person, modern technology such as Skype has made it possible to reach people I never would have met otherwise.

Who am I? I am a New Conversation! And I am very excited that I get to share my story and provide you the inspiration and support for the transformation of your life—past, present, and future.

These days we place so much focus on being aware of what we are thinking, feeling, and speaking while setting intentions to manifest the lives we want. While these are all important components, I believe we are missing one vital link: the condition of the energy and its grid within our homes and office environments.

The grid I am referring to is the Hartmann Curry Grid. Two scientists in the 1920s identified how energy flows—horizontally, vertically, and diagonally. When we meet someone, we connect with each other on the horizontal grid, when we pray and meditate we connect to the vertical grid, and the rest of the energy flows through the diagonal grids. Everything that happens in a space lands in the grid—love, laughter, tears, anger, abuse, violation, addiction, et cetera. My gift is actually seeing and feeling the grid within people and spaces.

A powerful example of this is the popular show, The Biggest Loser, where contestants go on a rigorous weight loss and exercise regime. A few years ago, the winner went on The Oprah Winfrey Show and confessed that he had gained back one hundred pounds in a very short amount of time. My immediate reaction was, *of course you did!* The old energy imprints and emotional behaviors were still held in the energy grid of his home. Does that make sense? The energy of his past experiences was impeding the flow of the energy of his new desires!

For this reason, when I am working in a space I make sure to clear the old energy of "what was" and recalibrate the grid so that the new vibrant energy can flow freely. I also activate the nine sections of the Feng Shui BaGua in order to assist individual(s) in manifesting their goals, dreams, and aspirations.

The 9-section grid referred to as the Bagua addresses the nine main aspects of one's life, namely, Career/Mission, Knowledge/ Self-Improvement, Family/Community, Abundance/Money/Power, Fame/Reputation/Vision, Love/Partnership, Children/Creativity/ Goals, Helpful People/Target Market, and Health/Heart of Chi.

Feng Shui literally means "wind and water," and its purpose is to create balance and flow within your space. For example, take a gentle stroll clockwise around your home from the front door and pretend that you are water. Can you flow easily or is there a lot of stuff on the floor blocking it? Make note of the things that are impeding the flow for the purpose of removing it and opening up the energy flow.

Now, pretend that you are wind. What do you see in front of you... stacks of paper, cluttered countertops, disorganized book shelves, laundry that needs to be put away, or old, worn furniture? Are there items within your home that remind of you of an individual who has hurt or angered you? If so, make note of these items so they can be addressed and resolved.

Allow me to tell you a story of Mary Katherine, a client I worked with fifteen years ago. She called me in specifically to assist her in attracting a life partner. Immediately, I knew I would first be looking at the Love and Partnership quadrant, which is located in the back right hand section of the property, in the home and within each room and evaluate the state of energy flow.

When I did, I found a large storage shed on the property; it was falling down and literally filled with junk. *Action Required: Clear out and tear down storage shed.* While in the house, I noticed that the Master bedroom was located in this quadrant. Mary Katherine was using it for storage and it was a cluttered mess. *Action Required: clear out and move her bedroom back to this area.*

When I analyzed it room by room, I noticed that Love and Partnership quadrant in each room was filled with stacks of papers, books, boxes, et cetera. *Action Required: clear out and open up the flow of energy.*

I shared my findings and the actions steps required to get the energy aligned and flowing to assist her in her manifestation and was thrilled to find Mary Katherine was excited to get to work.

Less than six months later, I received my favorite kind of phone call. It was Mary Katherine, and she was beaming with joy! Within the first month of our session she had done everything I suggested, and by month three she had met her sweetheart. They are still happily married today.

In addition to my one-on-one work with clients, I love providing clearing and balancing processes on my website so that people can do their own clearing and feng shuiing. One of my favorites is the Flower Blessing Plate ritual so that one can begin completing the old energy and invite the new energy flow into the grid. As I mentioned earlier, this is the missing link to our overall sense of happiness and well-being. I am living proof!

Feng shui is not a quick fix, but an ongoing practice that will change your life. I am grateful to assist my clients and you in manifesting your goals, dreams, and aspirations!

ABOUT THE AUTHOR: Many refer to Stacy Davenport's work as a "new conversation". Stacy is a Certified Feng Shui expert specializing in Life Coaching, Life Purpose Hand Analysis, and Akashic Record consulting. The majority of her clients come to her through referrals, who as a result of her work have seen life-changing shifts in the energy of their home and work environments. Stacy understands that everyone will face challenges in at least one aspect of their lives—relationships, health, career, or finances —and she uses her tools to clear the energy of "what was" and create room for new energy that will allow her clients to manifest what they desire. With over twenty years' experience, Stacy has become known throughout the world as The Energy Catalyst.

Stacy Davenport, CPCC
Certified Feng Shui Expert and Life Coach
stacydavenport.com
stacy@stacydavenport.com
512-740-8101

Rather than Why, Ask How
Anitra Richardson

I was in my home office working when I suddenly heard someone crying in the other room. I ran out to see what was happening and found my twelve-year-son Jory with tears streaming down his face.

"Honey, what's wrong?"

"Oh, it's nothing," he replied, clearly embarrassed that I'd caught him, "Just my toe that I stubbed last night, it really hurts."

I could tell he was not telling me the real reason for his tears. "Honey, really, what's the matter? You can tell me."

His eyes welling up again, Jory told me about a YouTube video he'd seen—a man's heart-wrenching tribute to his four-year-old son, who had died from cancer. For Jory, the video had churned up old fears from when I had gone through my own bout of breast cancer several years earlier.

Jory was just five years old when I became ill, and this video had cracked his heart and opened the wellspring of sadness that had been locked away.

"Mommy," he said, his breath catching in his throat, "why does God let children get cancer?"

And there it was—the hardest question that I, as a mother of faith, dreaded. Realizing that anything I told him would sound woefully inadequate, I just held him in my arms and let him cry.

After a few minutes, Jory calmed down, but the incident got me thinking of my childhood, one dramatically different than the one my husband and I are able to provide for Jory and our daughter Marnee. Our home is a safe place for them to have needs, express feelings, and make mistakes—completely different from the chaos I grew up in as a result of the intense post-traumatic stress syndrome suffered by my parents. My mother, a Korean immigrant, was just five years old when her parents and most of her family were gunned down during the Korean War. By the age of ten she'd struck out on her own, eventually meeting and marrying my American father. A severe alcoholic and Vietnam War veteran, he was battling his own demons. They weren't bad people, they were just not able to provide the stable environment a child needs to thrive.

Yet somehow, no matter what else was going on, my mom managed to get me on a church bus every Sunday, where a kind person gave me donut holes and took me to Sunday school. There, I learned the story of Jesus and God's promise of heaven. I badly wanted heaven because, young as I was, I realized I was living in hell. Instead, I was taught that I was not worthy of this light because I was a sinner and that the light had to be earned through great sacrifice. That would become my answer to the question, "Why do bad things happen?" This religious belief system, coupled with my parents' dysfunction, planted the seed of "never good enough" deep within my breast. I came to see tough circumstances as the obstacles I had to overcome in order to achieve "redemption." Suffering was my ticket to heaven.

So, I began to grin and bear it, all of it: the molestation at the hands of one of my mother's boyfriends and the son of her best friend; Mom's short temper and explosive anger when I made mistakes and how she would blame me for everything that went wrong; my father's drinking and long disappearances; my shame and fear when I felt his hand cupped on my preteen breast when all I wanted was to be held and know that I was loved and safe; my mild concussion and hospitalization due to my stepmother's driving under the influence; the four a.m. paper route my brother and I worked at the respective ages of ten and twelve to help Dad with household expenses; the long hours my uneducated mother spent cleaning college dormitory bathrooms because of my stepfather's refusal to work so that he wouldn't have to pay his own sons' child support; and so on. All of this, the betrayal and abandonment, were my cross to bear.

Finally, I had had enough. The hard work and sacrifice, the grief and the tears, they just weren't worth it. Heaven be damned, it was time for some fun! While running away from "never good enough," I stumbled through college, juggling my studies and an almost full-time job with binge-drinking and bulimia. My once-mild depression continued to worsen until one day I found my own existence unbearable. I just wanted "something like a truck to run over me" so that I could be put out of my misery. The shame of failing grades, excessive drinking, and suicidal tendencies eventually led to academic probation and a social worker's office. I stared blankly out the window with tears rolling down my face, unable to articulate that "I'm never good enough." Instead of resolving my feelings, I left with a semester's worth of antidepressants. They numbed my pain enough for me to decide that I would prove "them" wrong: I would show them that I was "good enough." I didn't need to make sacrifices and I didn't need God. I'd do it my own way.

Armed with my new mission, I began stockpiling achievements designed to prove my worth: first in the family to graduate from college; a job at a corporate start-up with generous stock options and benefits; a swift rise up the corporate ladder; a Mercedes; my own condo; trips abroad; designer clothes; expensive restaurants; a handsome, caring husband and two healthy children; and the "right" neighborhood. I was an avid jogger, quit my job to be the perfect stay-at-home mom and sent my son and daughter to the best pre-school. On the surface things looked great. The reality was that we were financially struggling, thanks to the dot.com implosion and subsequent recession. The reality was that I hated myself so much that I was using my husband as a "punching bag," constantly angry with him for anything that went wrong. The reality was that I had hit a wall because nothing I did ever seemed to be enough to make my life just right.

Suddenly, I was exhausted. I vividly recall how hard it was to carry fourteen-month-old Marnee up the small hill to pick up Jory at his elementary school. I was too tired to take showers. I was too tired to find clean clothes. All the other moms looked so perfect and together, while I was, to put it frankly, a "hot mess." I was convinced that they were judging me and avoiding me. A cancelled play date was because of me, not because the other child was "sick."

A small lump rose up under my arm. The oncologist called it Stage-3 breast cancer, but I knew it was something else. It was that insatiable monster born out of fear and anxiety. It was "never good enough," rooted so deeply in my breast that no amount of internal denial and no amount of external achievement could extract it. Actually, these tactics had only served to strengthen the "dis-ease" that manifested itself into cancer.

One morning, shortly after being diagnosed, I opened my eyes and saw a soft light shining through the blinds of my bedroom window. It was the most beautiful light I had ever seen. It came to rest gently on my face, and for one brief moment, I experienced a profound peace before the memory of my recent diagnosis hit me. "Oh, God!" I cried out in anguish, "How am I going to make it through this?" Exhausted, I closed my eyes and that's when the image of a small fragile bird alighting into the hands of God came to me. Then I heard God in my heart telling me, "I've got you, let Me show you the way."

That was the moment I put myself in God's hands and began to let go and allow. I began my allopathic prescribed treatment: chemotherapy, a radical single-breast mastectomy, and radiation. Even as I did this, I knew that I fundamentally needed to change something inside of me or I would not live to see my children grow up or enjoy old age with my husband. I went to see Dr. Carol, a dear friend and psychologist, and lamented about my struggle with the "why" of this happening to me. She counseled me to stop asking "why" and to start asking "how." It was the best advice I've ever received.

As soon as I was willing to stop wondering *why* bad things happen and began wondering *how* God would show me the way, an amazing thing happened: I saw a small light within my heart. As I began to follow this light, I began to see the people, the information, and the resources that I needed to rebuild my life.

Looking back, it is hard to believe I was that person: the self-loathing, desperate mother and wife on the brink of death. Since then, I have been on an amazing journey to spiritual wellness. The first step was understanding the reason I'd found myself face-to-face with cancer, and, just as Dr. Carol said, this understanding came once I stopped asking why and began asking how.

I now see how certain choices and perspectives led me away from God's light. I can see how I allowed other people's perspectives to shape my world into a sad, scary, and miserable place. I can see how the abandonment and betrayal by my parents caused me to doubt my own worthiness. I can see how no amount of partying, eating, and drinking could numb my personal pain. I can see how no amount of money or success or status could stack up high enough for me to escape my shame. I can see how neglecting myself made me ill. I can see how my huge heart led me to try and make the world better for everyone but myself. I can see how "never good enough" was robbing me of God's grace.

I can see how seeing my self-worth led me to self-love; and I can see how self-love led me to take care of myself before taking care of others. I can see how this self-care allowed me to thrive. I can see that as I thrive I am surrounded by the abundance of all that is good in our world.

As I hugged my son, I admitted that I didn't think God put cancer in anyone's life. I admitted that I didn't know why cancer exists in a child or anyone for that matter. I admitted that when confronted by bad things like cancer, we had two choices: fear or love. Fear has us asking "why?" Love has us asking "how?" Jory was quiet for a moment, then said he was now able to see God in that story he'd seen on YouTube. Though the story was sad, he saw how the child's spirit was in the hands of God.

When we are willing to ask God how, we will be led through the sorrow and pain to a place more beautiful than any of us can begin to imagine. I can see that even in the sadness and the not-so-good days, there are extraordinary and profound blessings presented to us in each circumstance. Rather than ask why God is not there, God's presence is revealed when we choose to see the how.

ABOUT THE AUTHOR: Anitra Richardson is a writer, marketing manager, and passionate church, school and community volunteer. Born to a military family in San Antonio, Texas, Anitra moved over a dozen times before finally making Austin her home. A breast cancer diagnosis at the age of 43 served as a wake-up call, transforming her life and inspiring her to help others on their journey to self-love and wellness. Currently, she is working on a spiritual memoir tentatively titled, "What to Wear to Chemo: My Spiritual Makeover in 40 days and 40 Nights." She also maintains an inspirational blog, "In Her Light." Anitra lives in Austin with her husband Joel, her children Marnee and Jory, two sweet dogs and a cat.

Anitra Richardson
Anitra Richardson, LLC
Anitraricharsdon.com
anitrarichardson@me.com
512-506-1207

About the Authors

**Are you inspired by the lessons in this book?
Let the authors know.**

**See the contact information at the end of each chapter
and reach out to them.**

They'd love to hear from you!

Author Rights & Disclaimer

Each author in this book retains the copyright and all inherent rights to their individual chapter. Their stories are printed herein with each author's permission.

Each author is responsible for the individual opinions expressed through their words. Powerful You! Publishing bears no responsibility for the content of the stories by these authors.

Acknowledgements & Gratitude

WE ARE GRATEFUL BEYOND WORDS and yet let us express our thanks here for those who grace us with their goodness and light.

To our authors, you have opened your hearts and souls to share your unique and powerful stories of transformation. We appreciate and admire you. Your tenacity, purposefulness, and gentleness of spirit are evident in your words and you will undoubtedly provide hope, courage, inspiration, and direction for those who read your stories.

To our team and behind-the-scenes consultants who give freely of themselves and their expertise and provide guidance and loving support as well as the wisdom of years of experience, we thank you.

To our editor, Dana Micheli, we thank you for your professional and compassionate insights, your time and commitment, and the beautiful energy you share with our authors.

To our trainers Jennifer Connell, Linda Albright, Kathy Sipple, and AmondaRose Igoe: We are immensely grateful to you for sharing your expertise, experience, and enthusiasm. What can we say? You're amazing!

To Lynn Scheurell, the gifted Seer who penned our Foreword, we thank you for the acuity with which you approach transformation and the depth of your commitment to conscious living and freedom.

To our friends and families, if we've done our job you know how much we value your love, support, and heart connection. Thank you for inspiring us and assisting us through the years. We love you all.

Above all, we're grateful for our Source connection and the pulling of the messages of our hearts. As we continue to heed, you continue to provide. Namaste`

With much love and deep gratitude,
Sue Urda and Kathy Fyler

About Sue Urda and Kathy Fyler

Sue and Kathy have been friends for 27 years and business partners since 1994. They have received awards and accolades for their businesses over the years and they love their latest venture into anthology book publishing where they provide a forum for women to achieve their dreams of becoming published authors.

Their pride and joy is Powerful You!, which they claim is a gift from Spirit. They love traveling the country producing meetings and tour events to gather women for business, personal, and spiritual growth. Their greatest pleasure comes through connecting with the many inspiring and extraordinary women who are a part of their network.

The strength of their partnership lies in their deep respect, love, and understanding of one another as well as their complementary skills and knowledge. Kathy is a technology enthusiast and free-thinker. Sue is an author and speaker with a love of creative undertakings. Their respect, appreciation, and love for each other are boundless.

Together their energies combine to feed the flames of countless women who are seeking truth, empowerment, joy, peace, and connection with themselves, their own spirits and other women.

Reach Sue and Kathy:
Powerful You! Inc.
973-248-1262
info@powerfulyou.com
powerfulyou.com
powerfulyoupublishing.com

Powerful You! Women's Network Networking with a Heart

OUR MISSION is to empower women to find their inner wisdom, follow their passion and live rich, authentic lives.

Powerful You! Women's Network is founded upon the belief that women are powerful creators, passionate and compassionate leaders, and the heart and backbone of our world's businesses, homes, and communities.

Our Network welcomes all women from all walks of life. We recognize that diversity in our relationships creates opportunities.

Powerful You! creates and facilitates venues for women who desire to develop connections that will assist in growing their businesses. We aid in the creation of lasting personal relationships and provide insights and tools for women who seek balance, grace and ease in all facets of life.

Powerful You! was founded in January 2005 to gather women for business, personal and spiritual growth. Our monthly chapter meetings provide a space for collaborative and inspired networking and 'real' connections. We know that lasting relationships are built through open and meaningful conversation, so we've designed our meetings to include opportunities for, discussions, masterminds, speakers, growth, and gratitude shares.

Follow us online:
Twitter: @powerfulyou
www.facebook.com/powerfulyou

Join or Start a Chapter for
Business, Personal & Spiritual
Growth

powerfulyou.com

Powerful You! Publishing
Sharing Wisdom ~ Shining Light

Are You Called to be an Author?

If you're like most people, you may find the prospect of writing a book daunting. Where to begin? How to proceed? No worries! We're here to help.

Whether you choose to write your own book, contribute to an anthology, or be part of our how-to book series, we'll be your guiding light and biggest supporter. If you've always wanted to be an author, and you can see yourself partnering with a publishing company that has your best interest at heart and with expertise to back it up, we're the publisher for you.

We provide personalized guidance through the writing and editing process. We offer complete publishing packages and our service is designed for an outstanding authoring experience.

We are committed to helping individuals express their voices and shine their lights into the world. Are you ready to start your journey as an author? Do it with Powerful You! Publishing.

Powerful You! Publishing
973-248-1262
powerfulyoupublishing.com

About Lynn Scheurell

Lynn Scheurell is an authority on accelerating transformation for high-potential entrepreneurs in life and business. By decoding their personal energy patterns and dynamics, Lynn helps entrepreneurs make more informed choices from a place of personal power and awareness.

Since 1998, as the Creative Catalyst, she has been honored to guide thousands of visionary entrepreneurs to achieve their potential, help more people and change the world by starting within; the 'new' entrepreneurs know that personal commitment is the secret sauce that changes the world. By translating the opportunity for personal growth into conscious awareness, forward-thinking entrepreneurs can explore and actualize their potential—from their leading edge— to step into living their best life.

Her unique blend of highly developed sensitivity, extensive metaphysical training over more than two decades and positive energy gives her a unique perspective to discover and illuminate life truths.

Currently residing in Las Vegas, NV, Lynn knows she is successful by the degree of positive change she facilitates in, for, through and with other people, including her amazing clients – and she joyfully celebrates success daily.

Lynn Scheurell
Seer, Teacher, Writer
Las Vegas, NV
MyCreativeCatalyst.com

You are Powerful Beyond Measure

Share Your Power and Shine Your Light!